# Oh Lord,

# What Have I Gotten Myself Into?

# Oh Lord,

# What Have I Gotten Myself Into?

# LaMoin Cunningham

Pleasant Word

A Division of WINEPRESS PUBLISHING

Printed in the United States of America

Packaged by Pleasant Word, a division of WinePress Publishing, PO Box 428, Enumclaw, WA 98022. The views expressed or implied in this work do not necessarily reflect those of Pleasant Word, a division of WinePress Publishing. Ultimate design, content, and editorial accuracy of this work are the responsibilities of the author.

All scripture references are taken from the King James Version of the Bible.

ISBN 1-4141-0116-3
Library of Congress Catalog Card Number: 2004100192

# Dedication

I lovingly dedicate this book to my wonderful husband, Bill Cunningham, and to my beloved children: Wyvonna, Shaleen, and Greg.

# Table of Contents

# Acknowledgements

*I* am so thankful to my late mother, Hazel Hagar, for all of her encouragement to me in writing this book. I only regret that she went home to be with Jesus two years before it went to print.

I thank my grandson, Shane Cunningham, for helping me with the computer when there were times I wanted to burn the documents and throw the computer against the wall.

I am also grateful to friends, Tom Fowler and John Yingling, for helping me with computer tasks. They have graciously given their time and instruction to me while trying to get my manuscript to the publisher.

I want to thank Angie Nichols for taking the time to read and correct the manuscript.

I wish to thank my children who have encouraged me to complete the book. It also serves as a legacy to them because it tells the story of my life and our mission experiences.

Above all, I thank my husband, Bill, who has loved me through all of these years and all of my moods while writing. He has been the major source of encouragement to me. Writing a book requires a lot of commitment and work. There were times when discouragement almost won, but Bill continued to praise me and to cheer me on to finish the book.

# Introduction

This book is intended to simply open up my factual and unpretentious memories as a twenty-four year-old missionary wife and mother of three young children.

My mother always wanted me to write about my experiences, but I didn't think anyone would be interested in reading another missionary book. Then I started to notice that there were very few books written by missionaries. I certainly don't consider myself to be an outstanding missionary. Many others have sacrificed more, endured more, and accomplished more in a short time than I will do in my life, but in forty years of missionary work, I have had some interesting experiences.

I love to tell of all the adventures of our work. Friends have listened with interest and said, "You should write a book." Well, here it is. I do hope you enjoy it. It is not written with the purpose for me to be a spiritual guide or teacher. I am a missionary because God saw fit to choose me for that purpose, and I obeyed. I am not super spiritual. I have tried to portray in these pages that I have the same emotions as any other woman. I hurt, cry, laugh; am weak; become discouraged, tempted, angry, lose faith, question God, and yell at my kids—just like you do (at least I hope some of you do, because I would hate to think that I am the only mother who did that).

I try, in my life and in my writing, to be transparent. I am not much, but what I am is by the grace of God. I feel that we miss many opportunities to minister to others by wearing our masks of perfection. I removed mine years ago.

I don't mind if others see my weaknesses if it will help to comfort some other Christian. I want people to be blessed by my life—not intimidated.

I feel that we all need to laugh more in this stressful age in which we live. The Bible says, "A merry heart doeth good like a medicine: but a broken spirit drieth the bones" (Proverbs 17:22). I have tried to portray my experiences with humor and interest to entertain you for a couple of hours. I never intended to write a serious, pious story about my mission life. God must have a sense of humor, because we are made in His image. There is a time to be serious and also a time to laugh. I hope you will laugh at a few things in my book.

Some of the names have been changed in the book to avoid causing any embarrassment to any of my missionary friends. I have written the stories as I remember them, and if all the facts are not perfect, it is because of a bad memory and not done intentionally.

I pray that some missionary might be encouraged and strengthened as he or she is in the middle of full-blown culture shock. Don't give up. Hang in there. There is happiness after culture shock.

Maybe some of you who are reading this are running from the call of God to be a missionary. Please know that you don't have to be perfect to be a missionary—just willing. All you need to do is surrender and God will mold you into what He wants you to be and help you to accomplish the work that He wants you to do.

I hope it will help my readers to be more aware of the needs and burdens of missionaries and their children. Above all, please understand that missionaries are just humans like you—no better and no worse. We do make mistakes while we strive to be all things to all men and to ultimately try to please God.

My greatest desire is to be obedient to my wonderful Savior, Jesus Christ. I have never regretted making the decision to follow the Lord as a missionary. However, I do regret some of the results that were usually due to immaturity and lack of wisdom and good judgment. I regret that missionary life was very difficult and harmful to our children in some ways. They were not called to be missionaries and were on the field because of Mom and Dad. Like all parents, we made some mistakes, but I have to commit the good and bad to the Lord and let Him use it as He sees fit.

I also pray that some will be saved after reading my testimony. I would love to hear from you if you have enjoyed the book and have any positive comments about it. You can contact me at *BillLaMoinC@cs.com*.

# CHAPTER 1

## My Journey Began in Arkansas

*I* was sitting next to the window, stretching my neck, and straining my eyes as our plane made its landing approach. I was finally able to get a good view of the land below that would become my home. Fear and anxiety gripped my young heart as I silently groaned, "Oh Lord, what have I gotten myself into?"

It seemed that I was born to travel. I had planned and prepared for this particular trip for about three years, but now I was not so sure that I had made the right decision in the beginning.

When I was born in the very small town of Grubbs, Arkansas, no one would ever have believed that some day I would be sitting in an airplane that was about to land in the country of Ethiopia. When you view a sweet, fragile, newborn baby, you can never imagine what lies ahead for the little, innocent, new life. I know that my mother and dad, Arley and Hazel Hagar, would not have been so happy if they could have seen into the future. And I certainly had no way of knowing the experiences that lay ahead for me.

I was born in a little three-room, white-frame house on the main street of Grubbs. The street was about three blocks long, and our house was on a corner, right in the middle of the business district. The population of Grubbs was about 313, so the business district was not very big. It was in this little house that my adventurous life began on December 4. Since my parents already had two sons, I was a most welcome addition to the family.

The doctor had agreed to accept a rick of stove wood for his delivery fee because my dad had no money to pay him. We were poor! He arrived at the house that day slightly intoxicated. My mother was grateful that a neighbor (who was a nurse) was there to assist. It was really the neighbor who helped me to make my grand entrance. The old doctor had evidently taken a few drinks to steady his nerves and had succeeded in relaxing a little too much to do his job. Later, my parents learned that his medical license had been revoked because of his problem with alcohol.

He didn't even record my birth. When I was ready to start to school, Mother applied for my birth certificate and was very surprised to learn from the courthouse that I did not exist! It took time and witnesses to prove that I really had been born. My birth certificate reads "Delayed." Now, isn't that a fine way to start life?

## My Name Was in the Hat

Mother and Dad had discussed names for me but had never really decided on one. The nurse was French, and so she said to my mother, "Why don't you name her LaMoin? I had the name chosen for a little girl of my own, but I will never use it." Mother was delighted! She loved this French name. It was unusual and had a pretty musical ring to it. She proudly announced to the family her choice for my name.

LaMoin was definitely unusual for this little town of Grubbs. In fact, it was so unusual that Dad said no! Grandpa and Grandma said they did not like it. Other family members agreed with Dad. No one liked LaMoin. However, my mother had made up her mind. She still wanted to be fair, so she presented a solution to the problem. They would put all of the favored names in a hat, and the name that was drawn was to be mine. After each person had his or her turn at drawing a name, the name was put back into the hat.

The name "LaMoin" was always drawn. Everyone had previously agreed on Joyce for one name. Therefore, I officially became Joyce LaMoin Hagar. Although Mother agreed to put LaMoin in the middle, she called me by that name from the beginning.

## My Dad Was from Egypt, and My Mother Was from Cash

My dad was a handsome, intelligent man with black hair and olive skin. He had a "foreign" appearance. Many times throughout my life, people would ask him where he was from and he would reply, "Egypt." Because his name was "Hagar," they would say, "I knew you were from somewhere overseas." Then, with a twinkle in his eye, he would admit, "Oh, no. I was born in Egypt, Arkansas."

17

Dad was talented, loved to talk, and had a great sense of humor. I loved to listen to him tell stories about his boyhood and about some of his uncles. I have never had a great desire to trace my family tree because I fear what I might find on some limb. I know we had cattle rustlers, horse thieves, and convicts in the lineage. One of Dad's uncles was in prison for murder, but he really was framed and was released after the guilty man made a deathbed confession.

My dad worked hard to make a living. My grandfather had been a stubborn and ignorant man who thought that a formal education was not important. He kept his children at home to work. Therefore, my poor dad had to go through life with a second-grade education. It made life hard for him and for our whole family.

My pretty, black-haired mother married my dad when she was eighteen. She had been born and reared in the same house in Cash, Arkansas. Her father was a farmer who always provided well for his family. He was also the Justice of the Peace and a deacon in the church they attended. Therefore, my mother had lived a very secure and sheltered life. She loved life, friends, and fun. Mother was only twenty by the time she had given birth to my brothers, Maurice and Marlin, who are four and five years older than I am.

As far back as I can remember, life for us was difficult in Arkansas. The year I was born was no exception. Dad worked mostly as a farm laborer, but in the winter there wasn't much work. At that time, if a man was out of work, there was no unemployment money, no welfare, and no way to put food on the table, pay rent, and heat a house.

## My First Trip

When I was six weeks old, my father was facing another winter without a job and no way to support his growing family. The country was recovering from the Great De-
pression, but my parents were feeling no relief.

Dad heard that he could make money in Florida by
working in the fruit harvest. He sold the few belongings
that they had accumulated, loaded an old pickup truck,
and started to Florida. My grandparents and uncle went
with us. Can you imagine five adults, two children, and a
baby riding one thousand miles in a pickup truck? People
wouldn't consider doing it today. The old truck also had
bad tires and Dad patched twenty-six flat tires on that
memorable trip to the Sunshine State.

Dad got a job on a farm, and we moved into a house.
Mother and Dad managed to establish a pretty good life,
and they loved Florida. After three years, the war started
and Dad was drafted. He was to be inducted in Jacksonville, Florida. My relatives had returned home earlier, and
Dad did not want to leave his wife and young children alone.
He got the draft board to change his induction center to
Little Rock and returned to Arkansas. By this time, I was
about three years old.

It was back in Arkansas that, to Dad's surprise, he didn't
pass the physical examination for active duty in the Army.
Again he faced the future without a job, as did many men
who were out of work at that time.

After a few unsuccessful months of trying to find steady
work, my parents decided to go to California, where
Mother's brother lived. I was barely four years old when we

boarded the Greyhound bus for the long ride from Arkansas to Los Angeles. When we arrived in LA, Dad had no problem finding a job, but housing was another story.

## No Vacancies

Even though I was very young, I can remember how my mother and aunt searched daily for an apartment. I remember the disappointment at the end of each day when the only answers they received were "no vacancies."

We were blessed to be able to temporarily live with my uncle and aunt. During those war years, many people slept in their cars or out in the open. The problem of "homeless people" is not new.

Someone told my mother about an apartment that was being vacated. She literally ran to the owner before someone else could beat her to it. It had not been rented! The lady said she would rent it to Mother and she was ecstatic. Suddenly her joy turned into fear. She thought, "Oh, no. I haven't told her that I have three children." Not only was there a shortage of housing, but landlords did not want to rent to people with children. Others had confronted Mother with this attitude, and out of desperation and anger, she retorted to one landlord, "Well, I guess I'll just have to go home and drown the kids!"

Mother could hardly believe her ears! We finally had a place to live.

We had a pretty good life in LA, but I can remember how Dad feared for his family because of the violent conditions there. Crime was rampant. We had no car, so we always rode in the streetcars. We had to walk about two blocks from our apartment to board the streetcar. There wasn't much traffic in that quiet neighborhood. It was a good place for crime. Many people were mugged and robbed near the hedges that lined the sidewalk, so Dad always made us walk in the middle of the street at night.

We were in LA when the war ended. I remember all the sirens and other noise as the city celebrated the end of World War II. Confetti was knee-deep in the street. Strangers were hugging and kissing each other. The city went wild.

I was six years old when Dad decided that we were returning to Arkansas. He feared raising his children in the city of Los Angeles. He did not want us to be in an environment where our associations might lead us astray.

## Dad Ruined My Movie Career

Many things contributed to Dad's fears, but I remember one thing in particular that helped him to make his decision to leave Los Angeles. I was playing outside one day when a man passed and looked my way. He was a talent scout for the movies. He immediately came to Dad and begged his permission to train me to dance and act. Dad refused.

"Your little daughter is beautiful and just the type we Hollywood agents look for. I can train her to dance and to act. Why, she can be a star. She will be able to have money and any man she wants!"

My dad had a pretty bad temper. This proposal only succeeded in making him angry enough to order the man from our house. "Get out of my house before I throw you out. You are not turning my daughter into a Hollywood dancer." There went my possible movie career! There was to be no discussion—ever!

Many times the fleeting thought has entered my mind that if Dad had not been so stubborn I may have had the opportunity to be rich and famous. Maybe I would have been a star. However, I think God intervenes in our lives, even before we are saved. If my unsaved daddy had been "star struck" and granted that talent scout's request, my life would have been so different. Maybe I would never have met the Lord Jesus Christ. It is doubtful that I would have been sitting in that airplane asking, "Oh, Lord. What have I gotten myself into?" Maybe I would have asked that question many times in my life but under very different circumstances. I thank God that Dad said no.

We boarded another Greyhound bus and headed back to Arkansas where we would be safer but definitely poorer. We returned to Grubbs, my birth town. We lived with my grandparents until Dad was able to get a job and a house.

## I Didn't Want to Go to School

It was now time for me to start to school. We lived about three blocks from the school. Two of my cousins, Jim and Evelyn, were my age. They had already started to school, so Mother thought that I wouldn't mind going since I would be in their room. Wrong!

She dressed me in a pretty summer dress, put curls in my long, black hair, and we walked three blocks down a dirt road to the school. When I saw the school, I made a decision—I wasn't going to school. I stopped in the road and started having my fit of resistance. Mother talked, coaxed, promised, and scolded, but nothing would change my mind. I was determined that I wasn't going to school.

She tried to force me, but I fell down in that dusty road and fought and cried until she was exhausted. After mixing my tears with the dust, I was a mess. Mother accepted the fact that I was not even presentable and that she would try the next day. We went home. I had won the battle, but I didn't win the war. After all, tomorrow was another day, and my mother was also determined.

We went back to school the next day, and Mother managed to get me into the classroom. My cousins were there, but I didn't care. I wasn't going to stay. The teacher, Mrs. Mirth, was so very sweet, nice, and patient. She did everything to put me at ease and to calm my fears. In those days, we had a desk and seat that was big enough for two people. First she asked me if I wanted to sit behind Jimmy. No. In front of him? No. Behind Evelyn? No. In front of her? No. As a last effort, she asked me if I wanted to sit *with* Evelyn. I agreed to that. What a brat I was.

But that wasn't the end of my struggle. I have never been one to give up easily. Every day for two weeks I went to the principle, Mr. Swain, and told him I was sick and wanted to go home. He was also kind and patient, so he would call my older brother, Maurice, and have him to take me home. Finally, the sad day came when I went through my routine and Mr. Swain said, "LaMoin, I don't think you are sick. You can't go home today." The game was finished.

Every morning, for weeks, Mother would put me on the back of Maurice's bicycle to go to school. He would ride through town with me screaming to the top of my voice.

Needless to say, he hated me for awhile. He was so embarrassed. Everyone would know that LaMoin was going to school. For years, every time I went back to Grubbs, the older people would say, "You're the one who cried every day when you had to go to school, aren't you?" My reputation followed me for many years.

## A New Baby in the House

When I was seven, Mother gave birth to my third brother, Jerry. After having lived with two brothers for seven years, I was ready for a sister. I was so disappointed when Jerry came; I ignored him totally. I cried and begged Mother to change him for a girl. Our neighbor had three daughters and had given birth to a fourth girl at the same time Jerry was born. I could not understand why they couldn't swap.

I finally calmed down and accepted my baby brother. Mother told me how naughty I was acting, and if I didn't stop that he might die. Even though I didn't appreciate him, I didn't want him to die. I did learn to love him very much.

Dad worked in the rice fields and made enough money for us to live in Arkansas until I was ten years old. We then moved to Florida for a short time. But work was hard to find, and we experienced many hardships during those few months.

Arkansas always drew Dad back like a moth to a flame. He knew that he would experience hurt each time he returned, but it was home, and he loved it. He felt more secure in his home state.

When I was eleven, we went back home but had to leave again one year later. We returned to California, to my uncle's home in San Jacinto. Dad found a job on a dairy farm, and we moved into our own apartment, where we lived for a few months. Then we moved back to Arkansas to care for my elderly and ailing grandparents.

You are probably wondering about our schooling and how we managed. Jerry and I always enrolled in school wherever we lived. Maurice and Marlin finally quit but against my mother's desire.

In those days, high school students had to purchase their own books. My parents managed to buy a set of books for Maurice in the ninth grade and someone stole them. It was hard enough to keep food on the table, and there was simply no money for another set of books. Maurice had no choice but to quit. This gave Marlin a great excuse to quit while he was in the eighth grade. Dad was sorry about it, but with his lack of education, he was doing his best. Mother cried because she had desperately wanted us to have an education.

Somehow I managed to roll with the punches, keep my grades up, and persevere. I attended thirteen different schools through grade nine. I lost count as to how many times I changed, sometimes attending the same school two or three times. I went to four different schools, in three different states, during the ninth grade.

## The Move That Changed My Life

I was fourteen years old when Dad moved us to Flint, Michigan where my life would be changed forever. Dad and my older brothers started to work in the automobile factories, and for the first time in most of my life, we were able to enjoy some of the things that other middle-class people enjoyed.

When we arrived in Flint, I was in the ninth grade and had already attended three other schools that year. Mother managed to scrape together enough money to buy me two cotton dresses so I would look presentable, and I started school at Emerson Junior High. I was to try to make a place for myself among three thousand other students.

After the school year was finished, we moved to a nice house in the suburbs of Flint. In the fall, I enrolled as a sophomore in Bendle Senior High School, where I was able to remain until I graduated in 1958.

My older brothers contributed much to my high school education, and I will be forever grateful to them. There were many extras that Dad could not afford: senior pictures, class ring, senior trip, etc.; but my brothers made sure I had the money that I needed for these things.

I worked from the time I was fifteen so I could buy nice clothes. I tried very hard to fit into the social scene at school and to be accepted. This was not easy for a transplanted Southerner in this northern land. But my determination and desire had been strengthened by all the hardships we had endured.

In my junior year I wanted to be a cheerleader. I had never been athletic, but I needed the achievement and attention that I saw in the cheerleaders. I had the desire to be "somebody." I practiced very hard for weeks before the tryouts. With the help of a friend who was a cheerleader, I learned and practiced one routine over and over.

Finally the big day arrived for tryouts. Only one person was to be chosen. I was scared to death, but I had been taught determination and that carried me through. The other girls who tried out were better than I was, so I thought that I would never be chosen.

My performance was not great and I knew it, but to my surprise, I was chosen! Why? I was chosen because I was prettier than the others were. I would look better on the squad, even though I could not perform as well. Image is important, though so unfair! The hard work had just begun—now I had to learn to be a cheerleader!

During my two years on the senior squad, I remained the worst athletic cheerleader in the group, but I compensated with my mouth. I ranked among the top in school spirit, enthusiasm, and the ability to be heard.

Please, dear reader, don't feel sorry for me. My unknown heavenly Father was preparing my life. Fiber, endurance, courage, and determination were being instilled in me for the future.

# CHAPTER 2

# I Thought My School Days Were Finished

*graduated* from Bendle Senior High School as number sixteen in a class of ninety-eight. I now regret that I didn't aim a little higher so I could at least have been in the top ten of the class. I had the ability, but I didn't use it to the fullest. I sometimes wonder how I was even able to accomplish as much as I did, but I think that God was already programming my life.

I was eager to graduate but had no intention of going on to college. I had no one who really encouraged me to go for higher education. Of course, my parents didn't have the money for a college education, and they were happy that I had just managed to graduate high school.

There was some doubt for a short time as to whether I would graduate. I was on my senior trip to New York City when I got into a little trouble. Naturally, we all had our instructions from the school principal. We were to obey to the letter, or we would be sent home early.

Three of my friends and I met some very nice young men from West Point Academy. We introduced them to Mr. Hudnut, the principal. We were trying to do the right thing, which later proved to be a mistake.

We went sightseeing with the guys, and we were about ten minutes late in getting back to the hotel. As a result, we missed the class tour to Radio City Music Hall. When we realized what had happened, we rushed to the Music Hall and met the class and one of the other chaperons. She informed us that Mr. Hudnut was back at the hotel, frantically looking for us and making arrangements to send us home on the next train! Imagine that! We knew we were in big trouble.

We ran back to the hotel and tried, in vain, to explain to him that we were not trying to skip the tour but that we were just a little late. He would not hear us and confined us to our rooms. He couldn't get us on an earlier train since we were scheduled to leave the next day, so we rode back home with the rest of the class. However, he was really angry and told us that our punishment would be that we could not graduate with the class.

We tried to make a joke of it and keep "a stiff upper lip," but he did have us a bit worried. After all, we had waited for twelve years for this event. Later, he cooled off and changed his mind with the encouragement of the other chaperon. He did tell everyone on graduation night that they almost lost some of their graduates to West Point! We failed to enjoy the humor, especially my dad.

I was tired of school by graduation. All I wanted was to get a job and make some money. I needed money! I still value money. I don't love it, but I love the choices that it can buy. Money doesn't motivate me—but poverty does!

I wanted to be an airline attendant. After all, traveling was in my blood, and I had already logged a lot of miles. I liked traveling then and I still do. To me, the next move is a great adventure to which I look forward with excitement and anticipation.

I had already seen much of America, but I wanted to see more. Naturally, I had never flown—we could barely afford to drive—but I had grown to love a challenge. Flying, to me, was another challenge. Let me remind you that air travel was not common at that time. I was told how dangerous it was and that I should not do it. Because of my love for challenges, the fear of flying was not even a consideration.

Shortly before my graduation, two of our star athletes, Gary and Ron, attended a church meeting one night. The next day they came to school and told everyone that they had been "saved."

I laughed and asked them, "Saved from what? I was saved once when a train almost hit me."

Gary tried to reason with me. "No, LaMoin, this is different. I am serious. Don't laugh. We heard that Jesus died for our sins. We asked him to forgive us and save us. Please come to church with us tonight and hear for yourself."

"No thanks. If you want religion, that's fine, but it's not for me."

I thought this was some new high for them (we didn't know much about drugs then), and it would soon wear off. But it lasted, and they persisted in witnessing to me.

We could all see the change in Gary and Ron. They were indeed different. They carried their Bibles to school and talked about Jesus. They were actually becoming dull and boring. Even the teachers noticed it and felt sorry for them.

I had been reared in a loving family of good people with high morals, but they were not Christians. I can't remember going to church more than a half dozen times in my life. I went once at Easter. Even then, I didn't hear what the preacher said because I was comparing my new dress to the other girls' dresses.

Mother had been reared in a Christian home but stopped going to church when she married Dad. When we lived in Los Angeles, she taught me to pray, "Now I lay me down to sleep...." She had a pretty voice, and she always sang church hymns as she did her housework. I still remember those songs and find myself singing them now, especially, *When They Ring Those Golden Bells,* which was my grandfather's favorite song. (Recently it was sung at Mother's funeral.)

It is not my intention to discredit my dear mother in anyway in this book. She was a wonderful mother and I loved her dearly. However, because of the influence of my dad and his family, she never passed on her Christian upbringing to my brothers and me. I had never been taught anything about the Bible. My maternal grandmother died before I was born, and my maternal grandfather died when I was a baby, so I missed their Christian influence in my life.

Atheism was strong on my dad's side of the family. Many times I heard Dad and my uncles making fun of some preacher or asking the age-old, dumb questions such as, "Where did Cain get his wife?" Christians were a joke in our home.

Rev. Jewell Smith pastored the Burton Baptist Church about three blocks from our home. He visited us once or twice about the same time that my school friends "got religion" in another nearby Baptist church. We certainly gave Bro. Smith the deep-freeze treatment. His church had a reputation for being a straight-laced church that didn't believe in anything that was fun.

At this time, my older brothers were professional country musicians, and our lives revolved around that lifestyle. I loved dancing, and I frequently went to the clubs where they entertained. I thought I was enjoying life, but something was missing. I remember thinking, "Is this all there is to life? If so, why am I here?"

My brothers also taught me to play poker and other card games. When we had their musician friends over, we would play poker until the wee hours of the morning. I loved it, and I was pretty good at the game. Gambling was exciting. If my life had not been changed, I would have experimented even more with cards.

# CHAPTER 3

# The Experience That Changed My Life

One day in April, before I graduated from high school in June, my friend, Lou, came to my home. "LaMoin, please go to church with me tomorrow night." When she did go to church, she went to Burton Baptist. However, she was not a regular attendee. She had a good voice, and sometimes the pastor (who was then Rev. Edmund Dinant) would ask her to sing at church.

"Oh, no thanks," I laughed. I was not about to go to that church.

"LaMoin, please. It won't hurt you to go with me."

"Why are you going tomorrow night? It's not even Sunday."

"They are having a revival, and the pastor asked me to sing. I couldn't refuse, so I agreed, but I don't want to go alone."

"Well, have fun. You are not going to rope me into going. You know that I don't agree with all of that stuff, and I don't want any part of it." She was so persistent that she finally broke down my resistance. I agreed to go, just so she would leave me alone.

That night, Rev. Jimmy Allen, from Garden City, Michigan (Detroit), preached hard on Hell. "Why is he picking on me? I expected something like this. Why did I ever agree to this stupid idea?" I felt so uncomfortable.

As the sermon progressed, I felt *so* scared! I was no pagan. I had sense enough to know, in spite of my lack of biblical training, that there was a God, a Heaven, and a Hell. After all, I was an American—living in a Christian country. I believed in God and Hell, and I had long ago developed the ability to almost close my conscious mind to the whole matter.

I was no fool. I knew that I would go to Hell if I died.

The thought of it had always terrified me. I hoped that when death came to me that it would be sudden. I used to say to my mother, "I hope I can be killed instantly in a car accident when I die."

Mother was stunned. "Why would you say such a horrible thing?"

"Because I don't want to know when I am going to die."

Now I was listening to this preacher who was talking about the very thing that unnerved me the most. I was one of the first people out of the building that night, vowing to myself that it would be my last time to ever expose myself to that again.

Thanks to doing a favor for a friend, I was miserable for the next couple of days. The words of Rev. Allen kept playing in my mind like a record. I could imagine myself dying and going to Hell where I would burn forever. I can't stand pain!

"Dumb preacher. Why did he have to scare me half to death and upset my fun?" The Holy Spirit was dogging my steps. I thought about it at school, at work, at home. This time, I could not successfully push the whole concept out of my thinking.

I had a couple of friends who went to different churches. I asked one of them, "What's it like to be saved?"

"Oh, it's wonderful."

That didn't tell me a lot. I talked to another girlfriend about it. I expressed that I didn't want to give up dancing and my other worldly activities. She advised, "Try another church that doesn't think there's anything wrong with those activities. My church doesn't preach against it."

Even to my unsaved mind that didn't make sense. It was either right or wrong. I wasn't going to attend a church just because they would appease me. I had to know the truth.

It was April—income tax season. I was working at night for a tax consultant—filling out tax reports for the public. Toward the end of that miserable week I was working, but my mind was on Hell. I had to settle it that night. I simply could not wait another day.

After work, I picked Lou up and hurried to the church. When I drove up, I looked at the sign that had brought a smirk to my face many times before. That night I had a different reaction as I read, "For whosoever shall call upon the name of the Lord shall be saved" (Romans 10:13).

Church was over and everyone was leaving. I parked my car, got out, and started walking toward the door. One of the teenage girls said, "You're too late."

"Not for what I came for," I replied as I hurried for the door.

I went to the pastor. "Excuse me. May I speak with you in private?"

"Sure." He excused himself and motioned for me to follow him to the front of the church. We sat down on the first pew, on the right side of the pulpit.

"I need to ask you some questions about being saved."

Pastor Dinant explained the plan of salvation to me in such a very simple way that I would have had to be stupid not to understand. I was not stupid. I did understand. But the devil was not giving up so easily. A great battle was raging within my soul. It was agonizing! I was not unhappy. I enjoyed my life. But I was afraid of Hell. The love of God mattered very little, but the wrath of God moved me.

After answering my questions for two long hours, Pastor Dinant said, "LaMoin, wouldn't you like to know, without a doubt, that, if you died tonight, you will go to Heaven?"

"Yes, I would. But if I get saved, do I have to stop playing cards, dancing, and all these other things that I enjoy?"

This was the clincher. I knew that if he answered yes, I would refuse to be saved, regardless of my fears.

Pastor Dinant was a wise man. Since he was a former New York gangster (a lieutenant for the notorious Dutch Schultz), he understood some of my feelings.

"LaMoin, all you have to worry about is getting right with God. Let those other things take care of themselves. Are you willing to ask Jesus to come into your heart?"

"Yes."

"Just bow your head, pray, and ask the Lord to save you."

I bowed my head and sat in silence for a few seconds, which seemed like an eternity.

"I don't know how to pray."

"I'll help you. Please repeat after me. 'Dear God, I know I'm a sinner. I am sorry for my sins. I know Jesus died on the cross to take the punishment for my sins. Please forgive me and come into my heart.'"

I repeated that simple prayer after him. The victory was won! The load of sin, which had felt like a thousand-pound boulder, was lifted from my tired shoulders! I felt as light as a feather! I was changed! I couldn't believe it; and words are not adequate to describe the unspeakable joy that entered my heart that night on April 10, 1958.

I felt like I was floating when I left the church. Something had happened in my heart and I knew that I was different.

As I drove home, I wondered how I would tell my family. I could have avoided telling them, but the springs of living water were gushing up within my soul, and I could not keep silent. My parents were sitting in the kitchen when I got home. I approached them hesitantly, not knowing what response to expect but dreading the worst.

"Mother, Dad, I got saved tonight."

Startled, they looked at me. "Are you sure you know what you're doing?" asked Dad. It seemed that he was asking, "Do you know what you are getting yourself into?"

"Yes, I am sure."

Mother didn't make much comment. I think she was stunned. It seems that I remember her murmuring something like, "I am happy for you."

The next day I had to tell my brothers. "Oh, no, what am I getting myself into this time?" I knew they would laugh and make fun of me. I remembered the many times we had laughed at others. But God was already developing strength in me. I knew that I could not prolong the revelation. They

39

would suspect something anyway because I already knew that I was different. I couldn't hide what had happened to me. I didn't want to hide it. I was so happy. I wanted to shout it from the rooftop. For the first time in a long time, I had been able to rest my head on my pillow in peace, not fearing Hell. Oh, how sweet it had felt when I went to sleep that night with the knowledge rushing through my mind and heart that I was going to Heaven. (In witnessing to people, I have been asked so many times, "How do you know the Bible is real?" I say, "Because of what happened in my heart when I did what it instructed me to do.")

My brothers were in the living room. I thought, "Well, here goes. I may as well get this over now."

"I got saved last night."

"You did what?" They looked completely dumbfounded. I am sure they were thinking, "What is she babbling about?"

"I got saved last night. I asked Jesus to forgive me for my sins and take me to Heaven when I die." To my surprise and relief, no one laughed. I think they were too shocked.

My life changed so rapidly. I didn't bring about the change, but the Holy Spirit did. I didn't have to worry about the things that almost kept me from being saved. The desire for those things left me. As spiritual knowledge came, so did conviction. Shortly after I was saved, the old gang came around.

"Come with us to the dance tonight?" one of my friends asked.

"No, I am sorry, but I can't. I am a Christian now."

"Well, if one dance can hurt your faith, it must not be very strong anyway. Why don't you just test it?" (Doesn't that sound like Satan?)

To my logical mind, it sounded reasonable, so I went. I was so miserable at that dance, and I would have left, but I didn't have transportation home. For the first time in my life, I could not enjoy dancing.

Before we left, I had already settled in my mind and heart that we would have an accident on the way home. I had really accepted the idea that I would have one of my legs cut off.

When I reached home that night, I walked into the house and closed the door. I could not believe it! I was still in one piece and nothing had happened! I remember looking up and down at my legs. The conviction was strong enough that I never went back to another dance. However, I know now that God would not have taken such severe measures to let me know that it was not His will for me to go to dances.

I was truly "hungry and thirsty after righteousness." I attended church every time the doors were opened. I dreaded to hear the closing prayer from one service to the next.

## They Called Me a Fanatic

My family thought I had gone overboard. I was a fanatic! Right in their home!

"It's OK to go to church if you want to, but you don't have to change your whole life," they cautioned.

My friends said, "LaMoin's got religion." I didn't have to worry about giving up my friends. Very soon, they stopped calling. I didn't even miss them. I had struck gold! I was completely enthralled with what was happening within me.

I severely cramped the fun in my family. I was a thorn in their side. They really thought that there was something mentally disturbed about me.

My mother finally started going to church with me. For my birthday, she gave me a Bible, which was my most treasured gift. I would read it for hours at the time. My parents told me how "so and so," whom they once knew or heard about, had just gone crazy by reading the Bible too much. They worried about me.

In spite of my efforts to overcome my poor and transit upbringing, I inwardly suffered a bit from an inferior complex. It had been difficult to fit into new schools and new places. I didn't have as much money, nice clothes, a home as nice as others, cultured parents, or location stability. Behind the mask that I wore, I felt that I would not be totally accepted with my peers, who had all of the things that I didn't have. I was also from Arkansas, which was enough to bring about intimidation in the North and in California. But after I was saved, the thought occurred to me one day that no one was better than I was or possessed more, because I was now a princess—a child of the King. It completely eradicated my feelings of inferiority. Since that time, I am comfortable with the very rich and famous, educated or uneducated, or the poor and despised. I hold my head high and mingle with the best or the least. I have had the privilege to meet some people and be friends with others who represent all classes of people—some who are very rich and famous (including Mr. Sam Walton and the king of Ethiopia). God has given me some amazing opportunities in my lifetime.

About three months after I was saved, a missionary spoke in our church. During the invitation, my heart felt as if it would burst. I didn't understand what was happening. I knew I was saved and was enthusiastically telling everyone else about it. Then the missionary talked about giving yourself to the Lord for full-time service. Well, this was so foreign to me, but, again, a force beyond me pushed me to the front.

I knelt at the old-fashioned altar and said, "Lord, I don't understand any of this, but I do know that I love You, and I am willing to do anything You want me to do." Uh, oh! Little did I realize that airplanes would be a great part of my life, but not as an airline attendant.

# CHAPTER 4

# My Surrender Brought Many Challenges

*I*knew that God was calling me into full-time Christian service. I didn't know what He wanted me to do, but I knew that I needed to prepare myself for whatever He had in mind for me. However, I faced another battle—my parents didn't understand. They were totally opposed to the idea of my going to Bible College.

"If you were a man, you could preach, but you're a girl. Just what do you think you are going to do?" I didn't know what I was going to do. I just knew that when I told the Lord, "I'm willing," that something wonderful happened within me. I had no doubt that God wanted me in full-time service. Where or what? I didn't know. I was just going to follow one step at a time.

Dad told me all that I could accomplish if I would just keep my present job (at Westinghouse Electric) and give up this crazy idea. My brother had just purchased a new Chevrolet convertible—white, with red interior. It was beautiful. Dad played his best card. "If you don't go to school, you can buy a car like that." Material things no longer motivated me. I felt like Jesus when He told the disciples, ". . . I have meat that ye know not of" (John 4:32).

However, I knew that the Bible instructed me to honor and obey my parents. But how could I honor and obey them and obey God at the same time? I was being pulled in two different directions. I had no peace the day I sat down, picked up my Bible, and opened it to Matthew, chapter ten.

As I read those verses, God stilled my storm as He said, "He that loveth father or mother more than me is not worthy of me, and he that loveth son or daughter more than me is not worthy of me. And he that taketh not his cross, and followeth after me, is not worthy of me" (Matthew 10:37–38). From that moment, I knew that I must follow God, even if it hurt my parents.

My parents moved back to Arkansas the summer of 1959. I returned with them, knowing that I would be going to college in the fall.

I couldn't find work when I arrived in Arkansas. Finally, three weeks before leaving for school, I was able to get a temporary job in the office of a furniture store. My parents still couldn't afford to help me financially. I knew that it was totally up to the Lord and me, but I had no fear.

The night before I left, Dad asked, "Why are you packing *all* of your things?"

"I will be gone for a long time. I will need everything that I have (which wasn't much)."

Dad still had not accepted the idea. I had stopped trying to discuss the subject with my parents, because it always ended in a verbal battle that I did not enjoy. A wall was being built between us.

"You'll be there six weeks and come home," he retorted. Uh, oh! Wrong thing to say! I would have died first!

"How do you think you're going to live? You don't know anyone there, and you don't even have a job."

"God said that He would supply all my needs." (As I wrote this, I closed my eyes and tried to imagine how I would have reacted if I had been in Dad's place and one of my daughters was leaving under these circumstances. It helped me to understand his feelings.)

Thank you, Jesus, for giving me a simple, childlike faith! I still had not learned the (intelligent?) way to pray: if it be thy will. I just believed God when He said, "And all things, whatsoever ye ask in prayer, believing, ye shall receive" (Matthew 21:22). I simply believed what the Bible said, and I had neither doubt nor fear.

My brother was visiting in Arkansas, and he agreed to take me to Springfield, Missouri on his return trip to Michigan. This was a blessing, because the bus fare would have really cut into my meager savings.

I felt sorry for my parents when we said goodbye to them, but my heart was rejoicing. I knew that I was doing what God wanted me to do. However, that goodbye was the beginning of too many painful goodbyes that would plague my future life.

## My New Home

In the fall of 1959, I entered the Baptist Bible College in Springfield, Missouri with thirty dollars, a lot of faith, assurance, and determination. My brother helped me to carry my few earthly belongings into the dormitory, and then he said goodbye and drove away. I had never been to Springfield, and I didn't know anyone there, but I knew God and that was enough.

When I arrived at B.B.C., I thought I had arrived in the courtyard of Heaven. I was too happy to be afraid of anything. I was in a place where everyone was heavenly-minded and almost perfect. Well, I was about to be educated—in a lot of ways!

I bought my necessary books and paid my first month's rent. Because of church funding, rent was inexpensive. I had enough money left for food for a few days.

The days passed and I had not found a job. At first, I was looking for office work because I had some decent skills and experience in that area. However, Springfield was the home for six other colleges and a university. A few hundred other people were looking for the same kind of job, so I soon decided that I would work at anything, as long as I made expenses.

I had enough money left for one more meal. (We could get a meal in the cafeteria then for one dollar.) I still believed that God would supply my needs, and I was just as happy as if I had good sense.

One day the phone rang in the dorm and I answered it. The caller introduced herself as Mrs. Clark.

"I need someone to clean my house. Do you know a student who would be interested?"

"Maybe. How many days a week?"

"Four afternoons from one to five. I will pay twelve dollars a week."

I didn't have to make her wait long for an answer—God had just given me *my* answer. I was thrilled to start to work for Mrs. Clark, and I worked for her for a year.

I'm sure you are asking, "That is all you made?" That was enough to supply my needs. One dollar and twenty cents for my tithe came off the top each week, and the rest was used for bare necessities. But, just like the widow in the story of Elijah, the supplies were always adequate. It doesn't mean that I could blow money. Oh, no! I broke my watch soon afterwards and I had it repaired. It took me months to catch up financially for the money I spent on that minor repair.

I was also learning the value of a dollar and how to manage money. I thank God for those trials. That training helped to mold character and endurance that I would need the rest of my life. (And to imagine, sometimes our children seem to think that I had it so easy and that I don't understand their hardships!)

I was so hungry to know the Word of God that I enrolled in all of the Bible courses that a female was permitted to take. I was still like a sponge—soaking in everything that I could hear about this newfound life in Christ. I studied diligently, especially in Personal Evangelism and Theology. I wanted to learn, but I had a second motivation— not to be humiliated in class by Dr. R.O. Woodworth or Dr. Noel Smith.

I memorized every scripture in P.E., sometimes under silent protest ("What do you mean, the whole passage?"). Dr. Woodworth, whom we affectionately called Woody, had a white patch of hair that stood up slightly on top of his head and laser eyes that seemed to protrude. He reminded me of a proud rooster as he strutted in front of the class.

At random he would call one of the students to stand and recite, and woe unto the one who didn't know his or her scriptures. He would raise his arms, fists clenched, face flushed, and bellow, "You don't know this scripture? How do you think you will ever lead anyone to Christ if you don't memorize these scriptures? I would be ashamed. . . ." And he would rave on until the poor student wanted to evaporate. Great motivation—to learn or quit! I chose to learn.

We lovingly compared Dr. Noel Smith to Elmer Fudd. He was a short, plump man with a round little nose that seemed to wrinkle as he would snort, "Stand up and share all of your first-year knowledge with the rest of the class. I know you first-year students brought all of the knowledge to school."

I studied furiously in Dr. Smith's theology class. One day, just as we all dreaded, he roared, "Miss Hagar, stand up and tell me about the significance of the Passover." I was one of about six women in a large class of men. I didn't have to be a rocket scientist to realize that he wanted to have a little fun that day, which seemed from his outward appearance to be totally uncharacteristic for him.

I tried to disguise my fear and to steady the tremors within me as I stood and expounded what we had learned about the Passover. Oh, how I thanked the Lord that my fear had motivated me to learn that lesson in detail! I was about half finished when he snorted, "Shut up and sit down. You know what you're talking about."

I will always be thankful for all of my training at B.B.C. However, a couple of classes stand out in my mind. One of these was English class, under the instruction of Dr. Paul Lupo. He instilled within me a love for writing and taught me so much about the subject. Without the training that I received from him, I don't think this book would be a reality.

I am also thankful for my speech classes with Mrs. Norma Gilming, and Practice Teaching under the instruction of Betty Hoverstrydt. In high school, I chose to take a letter drop on my report card instead of making an oral book report. I hated speaking before people. I suppose it was because of poor self-esteem. In these classes, I was required to speak to the class.

I remember the first time in Practice Teaching when I had to teach the whole class—men and women—as if I was teaching small children. Naturally, I was afraid. When I am afraid, I study hard. I prepared that lesson so well that I was like a machine.

I was teaching about the walls of Jericho falling, and I was putting a lot of action and excitement into my story. When I came to the point where the walls fell down flat, a man yelled, "Amen." I had not written that into my script, and I almost lost my memory!

That training was so very good for me. It must have succeeded, because now I love to speak, and it seems that I never have enough time to say what I want to say!

I worked hard at B.B.C., both in and out of school. I was used to sacrifice so it didn't bother me that I never had a spare dime to spend on luxuries. I had to trust God daily to meet my needs. I worked at anything I could get. I did house cleaning, ironing, and waitressing to earn enough for my personal and school expenses.

I can remember being so tired that I would have given a hundred dollars (if I had it) for a couple of hours of sleep. I was so tired when I dragged myself out of bed every morning that I was afraid I would go to sleep and drown in the shower.

I was completely absorbed in learning and was dedicated to my commitment. I didn't date often, for a couple of reasons. First, I had to work most of the time that I was not in class or studying. Second, I was not interested in a lot of the guys. I am afraid that I had become just a bit pious and felt that a lot of the guys were not as "spiritual" as I thought they should be. I had learned by now that everyone there did not wear halos!

A tall, dark and handsome upper classman, Bill Cunningham, worked in the college bookstore. (He was preparing to go to the mission field. Ugh!) He used to irritate me to the nth degree. I would go into the bookstore to look for a book, minding my own spiritual business, and he would approach me.

"I'm surprised that a pretty girl like you isn't married or engaged yet."

I replied rather indignantly, "God says, 'But seek ye first the kingdom of God, and his righteousness; and all these things shall be added unto you' (Matthew 6:33). If God wants me to get married, He will give me the right person." I didn't mean to be a prude, but that's how I really felt. I was taking this new life very seriously.

## Lord, You Can't Be Serious

Toward the end of my second year, that old feeling of strong conviction came upon me again. The Holy Spirit was fingering around my heart. This time I was not very thrilled! How would you feel if God told you He wanted you to go to Africa as a missionary? I felt the same way!

A flashback from my senior year in high school flooded my mind. A lady missionary had spoken to our class. (Can you imagine how times have changed? Can you see a missionary being permitted to teach a class of high school seniors in a public school today?) She had lived for many years in the Amazon region of Brazil. She related to us all the things that she had endured and how she had been expected to eat roasted monkeys, etc.

You can very well imagine how this impressed me as an unsaved, spiritually ignorant, wild-natured, fun-loving, luxury-craving teenager! Silently, I said, "Lady, you are nuts. That's the last thing in this world I would ever do. I would rather choose to push the button on the electric chair than to do what you are doing!"

Now, God was telling *me* to go to *Africa* as a missionary! "Now, Lord, I know I surrendered my life to You, and I told You I would do anything You wanted me to do. But really, Lord, I had no idea—a missionary? Now Lord, I know me better than You do, and I'm just not cut out to be a missionary. I think You'd better reconsider. I just won't eat monkey meat. You know what a weak stomach I have. I can't even eat spaghetti (I hate worms and spaghetti reminds me of them). Africa?"

I was more fortunate than Jonah was because I was in Missouri—a long way from the ocean. But I ran and ran. After totally exhausting myself and being indescribably miserable, I knelt beside my bed in my dormitory room one day.

I prayed, "Oh God, You know I don't want to be a missionary, and I don't think I can be a good one. But if You really want me to be, and if You'll give me the strength, I am willing to go to Africa."

Oh, what a wonderful, still peace that washed over my troubled soul. I had not felt that kind of joy since the night God snatched me from the grip of Satan and gave me new life in Christ.

# CHAPTER 5

## *Ministry, Marriage, and Miracles*

*D*uring my first year at B.B.C., I felt a strong burden from God for "Red" Foley, the famous country and western singer. He lived in Springfield—just down the street from where I worked for Mrs. Clark.

I had heard rumors that he suffered from alcoholism. Since my brothers were musicians, I had some knowledge of the entertainment world and knew that life could be hard in that profession. My heart was burdened for him. Just before Christmas, I knew that God was leading me to visit him. Realizing that it would be improper for me to go alone, I asked a couple of friends, Jim and Gigi, to go with me to see him. It was snowing when we arrived at his home and rang his doorbell. His wife spoke to me through the un-opened door. When I asked for Mr. Foley, she informed me that he wasn't home. I could not understand, because I *knew* that God wanted me to talk to him that night. I refused to give up. I suggested we go down the street and visit with my employers, Dr. and Mrs. Clark.

We did so, and as we left their house, I said, "Let's go back to the Foleys and try again."

Jim said, "But he isn't home."

"He will be this time."

We drove into the long driveway, rang the bell—no answer. I silently prayed, "Lord, I *know* that You led me here tonight." Still mentally refusing to give up, I walked slowly back toward the car. Before I reached the car, another car turned into the driveway. I stood and waited, because within me I *knew* who it was. Mr. Foley parked and walked toward us. He introduced himself and asked if he could help us. I introduced our group and told him that I would like to talk to him for a few minutes. He was so kind and invited us into his home.

He very graciously offered us chairs in his beautiful den. I quickly looked around the room and noticed that many gold records decorated his walls. I knew some of those records were the ones that I had listened to as a kid.

I explained the purpose of our visit. I told him that I was familiar with the music world and that I was very burdened about his soul. I couldn't hold back the tears that were stinging my eyes as I talked.

He said, "Young lady, why are you weeping?"

I said, "Mr. Foley, you are a famous man and a wonderful singer. You have blessed the hearts of thousands with your gospel music, which I listened to when I was very young. My grandmother loved to hear you sing. But I don't think you are a happy man, and I don't want you to die and go to Hell. I know that Jesus Christ can give you peace and joy, and I want to tell you about Him."

Mr. Foley replied with tears in his eyes, "Young lady, you will never know how moved I am that a person of your age would be so concerned about my spiritual condition."

Throughout the remaining two hours, Mr. Foley told us about the time that he had accepted the Lord as his Savior and what had caused him to get out of God's will— Christians! I believe with all of my heart that he was saved and that he is in Heaven today. His spirit was willing, but his flesh was weak.

After a wonderful visit, I thanked him for his time and hospitality as we prepared to leave. He said, "Thank you for coming. Your visit has meant so much to me. I want you to know you are welcome in my home anytime you wish to come."

"Shall I call first for an appointment?" I asked.

He smiled and said, "You didn't this time, did you?"

After summer vacation, I returned to Springfield to begin my second year at B.B.C. I wanted to visit Mr. Foley again. School had not started and only a few of the students were on campus. I went into the cafeteria one day and saw that handsome guy from the bookstore. I asked Bill to go with me to visit him.

When we arrived at his home, he asked us to come in, even though he was rushing to get ready to go to the train station. I thanked him but declined, not wanting to delay his schedule.

I never saw Mr. Foley after that. He died a short time later, but I knew that God had accomplished His purpose. I had peace in my mind that I had obeyed the leading of the Holy Spirit.

## I Accepted Bill's Proposal and Became Very Sick

That last visit to Mr. Foley's house later led to Bill putting an engagement ring on my finger and my promise to him that I could live with him the rest of my life!

When he asked me to marry him, I wouldn't give him an immediate answer. I said that I had to think and pray about it. He said, "Don't give me an answer until you can tell me that you will live with me for the rest of your life." To be honest, that scared me half to death! This was serious!

Before I was saved, my opinion of marriage was, if I get married and it doesn't work out, I'll just get a divorce. But now it was different. I knew that divorce was not in God's blueprint for my life. I agonized for a couple of weeks. I was advised by others to just break up with him and later see how I felt. But I had the feeling that if I did that, I would never get the second chance. Finally, I felt that it was the Lord's will, and I told him that I would marry him.

Shortly after we were engaged, I became very sick and entered the hospital with pneumonia. The doctors found that I had a lung disease called Bronchiectasis. It is a bronchial problem that affects the lung, making it deteriorate. I was told that surgery was the only cure. If the diseased portion wasn't removed, the disease would continue to spread to the rest of the lungs. They wanted to remove the lower lobe of my left lung. I refused.

Bill and I were planning to go to Ethiopia, East Africa as missionaries. I knew that the mission agency would never

approve us if I had a partial lung. Ethiopia is a very mountainous country, and it would have been very difficult for
me to live in the high altitude. I knew that God would heal
me. I still had that childlike faith.

I was so weak after leaving the hospital that I was unable to continue in school and work, so I was forced to
drop out of school and return to my parents' home. I missed
Bill, the college, and Springfield. My parents still weren't
saved, and we had little in common.

We decided to get married earlier than we had planned.
I had wanted to have the traditional student wedding in
May, but my desire to be with Bill and to be back near the
college was more important.

## Bill and I Were Married

We decided on a small wedding, and I borrowed a wedding dress from a friend. Our parents were not able to come
because of the short notice and bad weather, so we had
only friends from college in attendance.

On January 19, 1962, Dr. W.E. Dowell, pastor of the
High Street Baptist Church in Springfield, stood before us
in the Division Street Baptist Church (where Bill pastored)
and asked me a sobering question. "Do you take Bill to be
your lawfully wedded husband . . . until death do you part?"
I had not been nervous about this wedding until then.

*Until death parts us*? Under normal circumstances that
could be a *long time*! The thought quickly raced through
my mind, "Oh, Lord, what am I getting myself into? What
if I get tired of him?" (I had never dated guys very long

before I became bored with them—now I was marrying one!) However, I had prayed much about this decision and felt that it was God's will, so I answered, "Yes."

Pastor Dowell pronounced us man and wife. Afterwards, Bill gave him ten dollars and he returned it to us as a wedding gift. We were so thankful for his kindness because it was the all the money that we had.

## Our Family Increased Quickly

A couple of weeks after we were married, I started back to school for the second semester. I was determined to finish college. After a few weeks, I started to have an upset stomach. You're right—I was pregnant! I had a new husband, college, and now a baby. We were thrilled that we were going to be parents.

However, during this time an incident occurred that almost made me regret my decision to get married! A few months before Christmas, I wanted to put a gift on lay-away for Bill. Due to the fact that I had never succeeded in surprising my dad or my brothers with a gift, I assumed that Bill would be the same way. I went downtown alone and put a nice cotton robe, with green and black plaid, on lay-a-way. To cover my tracks, I destroyed the receipts so there would be no way for him to find out about it.

My mother was planning to come to Springfield when I had the baby. About a month before the baby was due, Bill said to me, "You know I don't have a robe, and I will need one when your mother comes. I think it would be best for you to go ahead and get the one out of lay-a-way, and let me have it now instead of waiting until Christmas."

I was emotionally picking myself up off the floor, as I physically remained cool. "What are you talking about?"

He persisted on the subject while I denied having the robe on lay-a-way. Finally, he blew me away.

He said, "OK, will it help if I describe it?"

I laughed and said, "Sure. It won't create a robe, but go ahead."

I am here to tell you that he described the style, color, and design! Since I had been studying demonology, it quickly occurred to me that I was living with one! I just stared, wide-eyed at him as I began to back away toward another room.

I gasped, "What have I married?"

He thought it was very funny as he tried to comfort me and convince me that he was not possessed. However, he could never tell me how he knew about the robe. He admitted that I had not given him any clues, but he said, "I just knew. I don't know how, but I did."

Well, after forty-two years together, I have accepted the fact that he sometimes has a strange ESP, which is stronger than my strongest intuitions.

I went through the winter semester, summer school, and into the fall semester. I missed two days of school during the nine months of pregnancy. I went to school one morning and delivered our baby that night.

Our daughter, Wyvonna Lynn, was born on November 10, 1962. She was the prettiest baby in the hospital, and Bill and I could not have been happier. I returned to school after two weeks (sitting on a pillow) to finish my course. I completed studies at mid-term and returned for my formal graduation in May 1963.

## God Performed a Miracle

After I finished my classes, I again went into the hospital for lung x-rays. It was a different hospital and a different doctor. This would be the third such examination, and they were not pleasant. Plastic tubes were inserted into each of my nostrils and were run down into my lung. After dye was put into the tubes for the x-rays, the ends of the tubes were taped to my face on each side of my nose. I had to lie very still, without coughing, while the x-rays were taken. I could feel the dye gurgling in my bronchial tubes, but I couldn't give in to the need and temptation to cough or it would ruin the pictures. It was torture. The doctor had recommended good surgeons to me, but I knew that I wouldn't need one.

"Doctor, if you don't find any of the disease in my lung, will you accept the fact that God has healed me?"

He laughed, "Well, it would be a miracle if that would be the result, because a case has never been healed without surgery." He used the word *miracle* in a condescending tone. He didn't put much faith in my belief.

He phoned me a couple of days later and asked, "Which doctors examined you before and made the diagnosis?"

I gave him the doctor's name in Springfield who had given the original diagnosis and who was a noted lung surgeon and also the names of the team of doctors and students at the University Hospital in Little Rock, Arkansas.

He said, "I would like to contact them and look at the x-rays, if possible."

I knew then that God had truly healed my lung as I gleefully asked, "Why? You didn't find anything, did you?"

He defeatedly replied, "No, there is not a trace of the disease in your lungs." But he had to check the history. It *had* to be a wrong diagnosis—not a miracle.

My brother-in-law (a doctor) even said, "If you ever had Bronchiectasis, you still have it." He wasn't a Christian at that time, so he couldn't believe in miracles, either.

I know, without a doubt, that God will honor the prayer of faith toward healing—if it is His will. I am thankful that in my case it was His will and it brought glory to Him.

# CHAPTER 6

## Deputation

*I*n February 1963, Bill and I went to a meeting of the Baptist Bible Fellowship in Jacksonville, Florida. It was there in the Beaver Street Baptist Church (with me in a borrowed dress) that we were formally approved by the Baptist Bible Fellowship to serve as missionaries in the country of Ethiopia.

The sacrificial years of college and my illness were now behind us. I felt so happy and honored that God was allowing me the wonderful privilege of serving Him and representing the cherished Baptist Bible Fellowship on the foreign mission field. I had finished my college course, been approved as a missionary, and I felt that I had almost arrived! Little did I know that I was just leaving.

Now it was up to us to raise the needed monthly support to go to Ethiopia and to sustain us there. We sold our typewriter to get the money for gasoline, loaded our clothes (which didn't take much room) and our three-month-old baby into our 1955 Pontiac and headed for Indiana. Bill was to present his burden for Ethiopia and need for support to our first church. Wyvonna's nursery was a car bed in the back seat. Our home was the car! Most of my life had conditioned and trained me for this part of our ministry—*deputation!* That word represents all the emotions known to mankind!

Deputation caused flashbacks to so many trips we made when I was a child, one in particular. I was almost thirteen, and we were going by car to California. Dad loaded the car with our few possessions, my mother, three brothers, and me. That was a miserable trip. We could not afford to spend the nights in motels. When Dad was too tired to drive, we would just sleep in the car for a few hours. Maurice, Marlin, and I were in the backseat with numerous "things," but the aggravation to me was Marlin's guitar! When he wasn't playing it and singing, the end of the strings on the keys were poking into my leg—all the way from Arkansas to California (before interstates)!

Bill and I are "faith" missionaries, which means that we are not put on a salary by the mission agency. We must trust God to supply our financial needs by visiting churches across America, presenting our mission field, and asking for financial support. Churches promise to contribute whatever their budget will allow.

However, all churches do not get involved, for various reasons. Maybe they have too many missionaries on support and have no money in the budget; maybe they are not really burdened for foreign missions; or maybe they don't like the way you comb your hair! When you have enough promised monthly support to take care of the family and the work, you leave for the field and trust God that the support is sent every month. If you still have faith after a year (or more) of deputation, you have passed the first course in missionary service.

The world (and many Christians) thought we had to be born brain-damaged to follow this lifestyle. But we were following a direct call of God to take the Gospel to Ethiopia. Don't get technical about how we know we are called. We just know. God speaks to the heart through the Bible and circumstances.

## I Didn't Know How to Be a Mom

I was twenty-three years old (Bill was thirty-one), a new wife, mother, and missionary. I had so much to learn. I had never been around babies, so Bill had to show me how to burp Wyvonna. She was born into this world with a personality of great determination like her parents. Unfortunately, she inherited my lack of patience.

We were excited on this first deputation trip—until we got close to our destination and Wyvonna got hungry. When she got hungry, she wanted a bottle in her mouth after her first warning.

Bill stopped at a restaurant to get her bottle warmed. While he was inside, she was screaming! I loved, cooed, patted, and talked as she screamed. Finally, I was bouncing her on my lap, trying to divert her until Bill came with her bottle. I bounced her a little too high and lightly hit her head on the top of the car, at which time, I recognized another family trait—temper! She was mad now, and I was a nervous wreck.

When Bill brought her bottle, I assumed he had tested it since he knew all about babies, so I jammed the nipple into her mouth. The quicker I could shut her up, the better. You're right—the milk was too warm, and she shifted into high gear! Oh, Lord, I didn't realize what I was doing! This beautiful little bundle of sheer joy was driving me around the bend. I was afraid I had hurt her and damaged her for life, so guilt kicked in. Bill said, "She's OK. She's just mad."

She screamed for the next few miles to the home where we were going to stay. When we arrived, our hostess took her, and she stopped crying immediately! It gave a great boost to my self-esteem as a mother! (Deputation that year stays in my memory as some of the "good ole days" that I never want to see again.)

In those days, we always stayed in the homes of church members or the pastors. That was fine, but it is not the ideal way to adjust to marriage and parenthood. We couldn't even fight normally!

We didn't have the luxury of disposable diapers, as all mothers do today. Before we left each home where we were staying, I had to wash all the diapers, sterilize Wyvonna's bottles, fill them with formula, and pack them in ice in the sterilizer, until we could get to our next meeting.

You very old mothers or you young modern ones are criticizing me by now and saying, "Well, if you would have been feeding her the proper way by breast milk, you would not have had to go to all that trouble." If I had been feeding her that way, she would have died of starvation! Again, we are forced to make so many choices!

We traveled thousands of miles, and Bill spoke in about two hundred churches. A lot of them didn't have money or didn't like the way we combed our hair! Most of the pastors and churches treated us as special people. However, there are exceptions in every situation. We encountered a few as new missionaries. This on-the-job training was requiring a lot of faith—and I was beginning to understand the term!

## We Met All Kinds of Pastors

We had a meeting in Mississippi. We were to stay in the pastor's home. Bill phoned him and sent him two letters to confirm our arrival time. We drove up to his home, went to the door, and introduced ourselves. He seemed surprised that we were there! (I don't know what his problem was; your guess is as good as mine.)

He said, "Man, if I'd known you were coming, I could have had some people at church tomorrow" (Duh!). It is so easy to place blame. Some people become experts at it.

His wife was putting dinner on the table. He showed us where we could wash our hands to eat. When we returned to the table, they were eating! I thought, "Oh Lord, what have we gotten into this time?"

He said to Bill, "It must cost a lot to travel like you have to do, with your family and all." (Jealousy?)

Bill replied, "Yes, it's quite expensive." After our meeting the next day, he handed Bill ten dollars and a "God bless you." I knew then that God would have to bless us if we were going to get to our next meeting in Rock Island,

Illinois. We didn't have to worry about gaining weight on that trip!

We were almost to Rock Island and realized that we were running on gas fumes. We put our *change* together and told the gas station attendant that we wanted eighty-seven cents worth of gas. He looked at us as if to say, "Wait until I go get my eyedropper."

Bill had saved fifteen cents to call the pastor. He went to the phone booth to call Bro. Rosenbloom, who was also the father of a classmate of mine. I had met him in Springfield and he was a real nice man. I prayed, "Lord, please let him be home because we don't have the money for another call" (which cost ten cents back then). I knew that Bro. Rosenbloom would treat us well. Bill came back to the car looking a bit dejected.

"Did you talk to him?" I asked.

"Yes."

"Well, what did he say?"

"He recommended some hotels and said he would see us on Sunday." (I think it was then Friday.)

I almost exploded. "Well, great friend and pastor he is! What are we going to do?"

"I don't know yet. Let's just drive around and let me think and pray." Bill said.

I knew we couldn't drive very far on the remaining eighty-seven cents worth of gas, but as I fumed and fussed, he drove into the parking lot of a luxury hotel. I read the sign, "Hotel guests only. All others will be towed." Bill ignored the sign and parked.

"You can't park here. They will arrest us!"

"Well, we can't sleep on the street. It's safer here."

He got out of the car and said, "I'll go in and get their permission to stay here."

As he walked toward the hotel I looked at my beautiful, innocent, dependent baby and wondered how I had gotten into this mess, and how God was going to get us out.

Bill returned and announced, "Come on. We're staying here tonight."

I thought about the commitment I had made—"until death do you part"—when he laughed and said, "Bro. Rosenbloom has reservations for us here." I felt that death was about to part us! I really did not share his humor at that point of time.

Bro. Rosenbloom treated us like royalty! We had the elaborate honeymoon suite, meals in the gorgeous dining room (all we had to do was sign our name), and a sizeable love offering after the meeting on Sunday—plus monthly support!

Bill was scheduled to preach one Sunday at the Landmark Baptist Church, where Dr. John Rawlings pastored. When we walked into the church, Dr. Rawlings met us, looked at me, and said, "You sing, don't you?" (I don't know how he knew that I *attempted* to sing sometimes—but not in a church with three thousand people.)

"Oh, no sir," I replied.

"Yes, you do. I want you to sing this morning, so run up there and practice with the pianist." Dr. John was a man that didn't take no for an answer.

I was stumbling through a song with the pianist and didn't realize that he was listening. Suddenly, I heard him say, "That's great! I want you to sing one for Sunday school and another for the broadcast." Their morning worship service was aired over the radio and reached thirteen states!

I said, "Oh, Lord, I can't do this." But I couldn't say no, so I sang—scared to death. I know what the apostle Paul meant when he said that he stood before the people in fear and trembling.

Bill also preached for the broadcast, and we received enough money from the radio listeners to buy a refrigerator on the field.

After we arrived in Ethiopia, we continued to receive money from people who had heard that broadcast. I'll never forget one offering we received. Just before Christmas, a letter with one dollar came from an elderly lady. She said, "Please don't think that we are spending all of our money on Christmas presents. My husband and I are old and living on a meager pension. We didn't even buy presents for each other. After paying our bills and buying food, we had this one dollar left, and we want you to have it."

Bill and I both cried. It seemed like the "widow's mite." God used it to teach us a lesson that we have never forgotten. We realized how much some people sacrifice so they might give to the Lord's work—and we had better spend it wisely!

## Another Baby

Wyvonna was seven months old when I became pregnant. I traveled for a few months, and then I went back to live in Springfield until the birth of our new baby. We paid about one hundred dollars for an old car for me to drive. It wouldn't start, so we put a new battery in it. Bill left for more meetings, and I tried to be content.

I lived across town from the college and the church that I attended. Soon after Bill left, I was driving home from church one night, and my car lights started getting dim. They gradually became dimmer and dimmer, then went out. I had to drive by the light from the streetlights, and in places where there were no streetlights, I opened the door and leaned partially out of the car for better vision.

I was so thankful to pull into my own driveway without an accident. Of course, the alternator had gone out in the car. I managed to get it repaired, then I decided that I needed to be closer to the college and church where I could get help if I needed it again.

There was a mobile home park behind the college, where a lot of the married students lived. We felt that I would be happier there, so we rented a small trailer, moved into it, and Bill left again. The first morning after he left, I went into the kitchen and was horrified to see tiny cockroaches crawling all over my countertops.

I called an exterminator and said, "Please come and kill these cockroaches."

He asked, "What kind of roaches are they?"

"What do you mean? They are just cockroaches."

"Well," he said, "are they English or German cockroaches?" (I was thinking, "Am I missing something?")

Now I was irritated. "I don't know what nationality they are. They are just cockroaches."

I was having a problem being by myself with a small baby and one on the way. I continued to have car problems.

Friends helped me to push that car all over that mobile home park, and it still wouldn't start.

Bill was three states away in meetings, and I wasn't getting letters from him. (We didn't use telephones much back then.) One day I had a fit of carnality, wrote him a letter, and said, "If you don't think enough of me to write, then this is my last letter." (He wrote—quickly!)

I was about seven-and-a-half months pregnant when I could handle it no longer. I wrote to my parents and asked if they could come to get us. Wyvonna and I went to stay with them in Arkansas. During this time, Wyvonna became very ill. She was about fourteen months old. The doctor admitted her to the hospital with pneumonia and inflammation of the stomach lining. We thought we might lose her. Another baby died in the hospital that night with the same condition.

I had an idiot for a doctor. One morning when he came into her room, I was crying.

He said, "You're going to Africa where you're going to see all kinds of sickness, and you're crying over this?" He almost became a patient himself, but God restrained me.

During this stressful time, I developed a planter wart on the bottom of my foot. This was due to ill-fitting shoes and not enough money to buy better ones. It was almost making me a cripple. I couldn't bear to put my weight on it. About six weeks before I gave birth, I went into the hospital and had the wart removed.

The doctor closed the incision with staples, and when I went back to have them removed, there was inflammation under one of them. He left it and told me to soak my foot in warm water several times a day, and it would heal. It did!

I went to the doctor who was treating me for my pregnancy, and he proceeded to remove the stitch. It had certainly healed. When he went in to remove it, I almost jumped off the table. It was like piercing my foot without numbing it. It really hurt. (Remember that I have a low tolerance for pain.) After he uttered a few choice words about the other doctor, he gave me an injection to numb my foot before he removed the stitch.

Shaleen was born on February 25, 1964. She was a beautiful, perfect baby, and we were so proud of her. When she was six weeks old, we said goodbye to my parents and brothers and started our trip to Ohio, where Bill's family lived. From there, we would be leaving in a few weeks for Ethiopia. I was glad that deputation was almost over and soon we could enjoy our little family in a normal lifestyle. (Normal? In Africa? I was trying to be positive.)

## The Beginning of Painful Separations

It was very difficult to leave my family knowing that it would be four years before I would see them again. I realize now that the parting was much harder for my parents than for me. Not only were they going to be separated from me, but also I was going to Africa with a "stranger" (Bill). They had not been with Bill very much at that time. And to add to the hurt, I was taking their grandbabies away.

After arriving in Ohio, we were told that we would have to wait until Shaleen was six months old before we could get her inoculation for Yellow Fever, which was a requirement before entering Ethiopia.

We rented an apartment in Canton, Ohio for four months. During that time, we did our last minute shopping for things to take to Africa. I'll never forget the day that we went into a shoe store, and when the salesman approached us, we told him that we needed his help. We had to buy shoes for our two small daughters for the next four years. We were blessed with a mature salesman with many years of experience. But even for him, it took awhile to choose enough shoes in the estimated sizes for them to wear for four years. The salespeople were always visibly shocked when we bought different items of clothing for four years. They couldn't believe that one couple would buy so much. We had many opportunities to tell people about our call to the mission field.

We packed all of our earthly possessions into fifty-five gallon steel barrels to ship to Africa. God had blessed our deputation and provided all of our needs. We had approximately seven hundred dollars in monthly support, our transportation expenses, and some money toward the purchase of a vehicle after we arrived.

When Shaleen was three months old (Wyvonna was fifteen months old), I realized that I was pregnant. I was almost beside myself, but not with excitement! This baby I was carrying would be born in Ethiopia—next door to the end of the world. Visions of horror now burst on my sight—now jungles and tree houses, no doctor and no painkillers, no clean hospital, and three babies to care for in the middle of a pagan land. But God gives a peace that passes all understanding, and He eased my fears as I committed my way unto Him.

# CHAPTER 7

## Goodbye, America

The long anticipated day finally arrived on Tuesday, September 1, 1964. Bill's large family was at the airport to say goodbye. I was excited as we walked up the steps at 5:10 P.M., to the door of a United Airlines plane that would take us to New York. There we would wave goodbye to America, "my home sweet home."

We dressed in our very best clothing (in those days, people didn't dress casually to travel). Bill wore a tie, suit, and a hat. I, of course, wore a new maternity dress. We looked like two pack mules! I carried Shaleen in an infant seat, along with my purse and a flight bag on one shoulder and a diaper bag on the other shoulder.

Bill carried a briefcase in one hand and a box of disposable diapers under his arm (we had splurged on these for the trip). On his left shoulder were a camera and a flight bag. A large, stainless steel thermos bottle, filled with boiled water for Shaleen's formula, was under the other arm, and he had one hand free to lead Wyvonna. Those seasoned travelers must still be laughing!

I had never flown before, and I was ecstatic as I looked out the window at the beautiful clouds, which looked like huge banks of snow. I had never seen such a thrilling sight. I immediately loved flying and still do.

Our plane landed at Newark Airport, and we were then transported by helicopter to the Kennedy Airport. I wasn't as fond of the helicopter ride, but I think I recall having tears in my eyes as we flew over that beautiful lady, standing with the torch of freedom high in the air, that we call the Statue of Liberty!

We reached the airport, checked in, and then started to the boarding gate. I was wearing high heels (go ahead and laugh), and we walked so far to board the next plane that I wondered why we had paid to fly! (You can picture us dragging all of our "stuff.") By this time, Wyvonna was tired, so Bill had to make room in his arms to carry her.

To make it worse, we didn't have the nice loading chutes from the terminal waiting room that we have now. No, no. Our plane was sitting as far out on the airstrip as they could get it, and we had to walk out to it. Bill was having difficulty carrying Wyvonna and all the other baggage by now, so a nice young soldier picked her up and carried her to the plane.

We were puffing up the steps to the door of the plane when we heard someone calling our name. We didn't know a soul in New York. To our surprise, someone from the travel agency had informed a reporter there, and they wanted to take our picture. (Missionaries were still considered special back then.) I was not in the mood to be honored by having anyone take our picture, least of all a reporter!

We later received a copy of those pictures—wow, what a mess! We were loaded to the hilt. My slip was showing; Bill's suit coat was pulled to the side because of all the weight on his shoulder; and we didn't look excited. We looked like the last rose of summer!

We went into the plane, and since we were in front of the line, I quickly chose a nice seat and fell into it. Bill put his entire load in the overhead compartment, then helped me to untangle the equipment from my body.

I breathed a sigh of relief. At the same time, my nose picked up an unpleasant odor coming from Shaleen. Kids can choose the worst times to go to the bathroom! I proceeded to change her diaper. (Now, understand that all of this action had transpired very quickly.) I was in the middle of my job, holding Shaleen's legs in my left hand and wiping with the right, when the flight attendant interrupted me to say, "I'm sorry, you are in the wrong seat."

"Wrong seat?"

"Yes, your seat is up here."

Well, remember that I had always traveled by trains and buses. Why couldn't I choose my own seat on this plane?

I gathered Shaleen, with the dirty diaper, all of my gear, and moved to the assigned seat, griping all the time to Bill. He removed all of our hand luggage from overhead and somehow managed to get all of it to our new seat. By this time, you can well imagine that he was also exhausted. We put our things in the overhead and collapsed into the seats.

A couple of minutes later, the attendant came and said, "I think it would be much more comfortable for you and the children in the bulkhead seats. Get your things and follow me." Well! I was about ready to send her where I didn't want to follow!

We finally settled into our flight, which was almost pleasant, except that they wouldn't give Wyvonna any extra food. She was sitting in my lap, and we had not paid an extra fare for her.

## My First Time in a Foreign Country

We arrived in Frankfurt, Germany at nine-thirty the next morning. Shaleen was sick, and we were advised to contact the medical center at the airport. The doctor said that she was just suffering from airsickness. He gave her some medicine and assured us that she would be all right.

We were unable to get connecting flights, so the airline put us in the Excelsior Hotel in downtown Frankfurt. It was nice to be able to rest in a bed again. I went into the bathroom.

"Bill, look at this toilet paper. Do they really expect us to use this stuff?"

It was worse than a Sears and Roebuck catalog! It was gray and stiff; I could see the wood grain in it! I quickly tried to turn a negative into a positive and I used it for stationary to write letters to our parents. Mother saved hers and gave it to me a couple of years ago. It brought back a lot of memories, and we can now laugh about it.

We walked around Frankfurt a little. I had never been out of America, so I was like a country kid in New York City. (I wonder how many tourists have been seriously injured there as they walked looking up.)

I had a lot to learn about traveling in Europe. One of the first lessons was that Germans don't put ice in their drinks. We ordered soft drinks, and a huge German waiter brought them to us. There was not a piece of ice in them! Now, I like my glass full of ice, so I asked, very politely, for some ice.

He replied in a very impolite manner, "They are already cold."

"But I'd like some ice, *please*." (He was about to step on my last nerve.)

He huffed back to the kitchen to get it, and Bill cautioned me not to start World War III. From the way we were treated, it made me wonder if World War II had ever ended!

I did think the hotel service was nice. The maid came into our room and turned down our covers before bedtime. The fluffy, goose-down comforters were about a foot thick. I liked them, but it reminded me of the feather mattresses that we used when I was a kid and the quilts that Mother used to pile on our beds in the cold Arkansas winters. All the heat we had in the house was a wood-burning pot-bellied stove in the living room. The bedrooms were like the North Pole, and we had so many quilts on the bed that it took great effort to turn over.

We had a good night's rest, breakfast in the morning, and headed back to the airport. We had a little time before boarding our plane, so Bill left the girls with me to go look at something.

In the meantime, I decided to mail my "toilet paper" letters. I was carrying Shaleen in the infant seat and leading Wyvonna. I stashed the "stuff" in a seat and went to buy some stamps. At that time, I didn't think about some- one stealing it, and as I consider it now, I don't think any- one would have wanted it!

I let go of Wyvonna's hand to pay for the stamps, and when I reached for her hand again, she was gone—that quickly! I looked around and almost panicked as I stared into a large, open part of the huge terminal. She was no where in sight! Instantly, my mind raced with scary thoughts. *Someone has stolen my baby*! "Oh, Lord, please let me find her."

I was half running with Shaleen in my arms, when I passed a man who was seated. Can you picture a pregnant, terror-stricken woman running with an oversized shoulder purse and a baby in a big, awkward, infant seat? (If you ever get real bored, just go to the airport and watch people.)

He said, "She went that way."

I ran in the direction that he pointed, around a corner into another big, open area. I couldn't see her anywhere. I hesitated, taking a deep breath before executing my next move—screaming! (I really didn't scream, I was just think- ing seriously about it.)

I turned to my left and saw a jewelry counter with a glass case. I looked through the case, and, yep, there was my precious twenty-one-month-old, Wyvonna. She had gone around behind the case and was calmly inspecting the jewelry. Bill missed all the excitement; I was so sorry about that!

# CHAPTER 8

# Africa, Here I Come, Ready or Not

During our flight from Frankfurt to Addis Ababa, Ethiopia, I was excited and scared. The mission field was about to become a reality, and I was about to become a real, live, walking, talking missionary. I felt old and mature for my twenty-four years, but as I look back on those experiences, I was so young and naive—even a little stupid! The Bible does say that we are fools for Christ's sake.

Thoughts of expectation were now crowding my mind. I thought I was totally committed to God's will for our lives. It is so much better when we walk by faith, not sight. I had a lot of faith. However, as our plane descended over Ethiopia, my sight of that primitive country temporarily overshadowed my faith.

I looked out the window and saw little mud huts, animals, and African wilderness. I groaned, "Oh Lord, what have I gotten myself into?" I was to ask the Lord that question many times in the future. I was committed to God, but

I was still scared. I remember a question that I asked many visiting missionaries who spoke to our missions class in college. Because of my mixed emotions I would ask, "Were you frightened before you went to the mission field?"

"Oh, no. We were just so eager to get there to win those poor people to Christ."

I was beginning to feel that there was something dreadfully wrong with my spirituality. However, Elmer and Mary Deal had come to speak to our class. They were veteran missionaries to the Congo. I asked them the same question, expecting the same answer. To my surprise and relief, they answered, "Yes, we were scared to death. We didn't know what to expect. It's normal to be scared." Finally, here were some honest missionaries.

I saw the Deals again a couple of years later. War forced them to flee from the Congo, and they came to Ethiopia. Mary was sick and went to my doctor. Part of her problem was abdominal gas because of the high altitude. The doctor said, "Just make sure you don't get around someone who is lighting a match."

Sometimes missionaries are afraid to show their inner feelings, fears, and weaknesses, because of the fear that they won't appear spiritual. They think people will criticize them. But I am not afraid to be "real." I think we sometimes discourage some who are running from God's will because they feel they are not good enough.

We were visiting in a church a few years ago and a lady came to me after our presentation. Mentally, she was looking at me on my pedestal of perfection. She asked, "Have you and your husband ever had an argument?" (See, she thought I was near perfect because I was a missionary.)

"Argument?" I replied with a smile. "We have fought all over this world."

My husband preached in the Sunday morning service in a small church and afterwards a man came to me wearing a very serious expression. "Do you and your husband ever sin?"

"Every day," I answered.

That reminds me of a missionary friend in Kenya who was entertaining a visiting pastor. They were driving in the city where the drivers usually pay little attention to the law.

Every time a driver would cut him off or almost hit him, the missionary would yell at him with a great degree of impatience. Finally, the pastor said, "Brother, you don't have much compassion for these people, do you?"

The missionary replied, "I'd like to see you come over here and live for awhile, then we would see how much compassion you have."

Missionaries are not super spiritual or unreal beings who are not affected by human emotions. We hurt, cry, laugh, get angry, discouraged, and fearful. We are tempted and demonstrate lack of faith, just like you do. We are just ordinary sinners saved by the grace of God and surrendered to the Master. We have felt a genuine call of God to go to the "uttermost parts of the world," to take Jesus to those who are lost and without hope. That is the only difference between the average church member and me.

## A Real Missionary Looks at a Real Mission Field

You will see throughout this book that I am real! I just hope you don't lose confidence in missionaries after reading it. People have always said, "Oh, I admire you. It takes so much faith and courage to do what you are doing."

Well, I appreciate the compliment, but it doesn't make me immune to the power of the devil and this human flesh. (I always try to keep my weight down so I won't have so much flesh to crucify! It's hard enough to deal with what I have.)

Our plane landed at the airport, a few miles outside of Addis Ababa. We managed to pick up all of our gear and the two children and leave the plane. As we put our feet onto that Ethiopian runway, we had no idea of all the experiences we would encounter during the next few months. During deputation, the missionaries are usually put on pedestals, but everything changes when your feet touch that foreign soil. You enter into stark reality in the nasty now and now!

Our professors used to say, "If you can't make it in college, you'll never succeed in the ministry." Truer words were never spoken. All the hardships that I endured in college were just appetizers.

I am so glad that God doesn't permit us to see the future. It would be impossible for us to cope. Did you know that you can eat an elephant one bite at a time? But if you look at the whole thing, it is impossible.

We received our first initiation when we picked up our luggage. The agent informed us that we owed seventy dollars for overweight baggage (I thought we had it all strapped on us). Seventy dollars? That was a lot of money in 1964. Our promised support was a grand total of seven hundred dollars a month. If our luggage was overweight, why didn't they charge us in Frankfurt? We argued, pleaded, got mad, and then paid seventy dollars. Welcome to Ethiopia!

It was strange, and a little scary, to see soldiers with rifles standing guard throughout the terminal. I almost felt that I had landed in a war zone. That feeling was to become fact later.

After we cleared customs and immigration, we walked out to be welcomed by many familiar faces. Many of the missionaries from our mission were there to meet us. Most of them were friends who had attended Bible College with us. Ethiopia was a newly opened field, and the oldest missionaries had preceded us by not more than two years. It was great to be among friends.

Lonnie and Georgine asked us to ride into the city with them. We had gone to college with them, and they had been in Ethiopia about one year, maybe a little longer. They had two little daughters and a son. Kelly and Karen were with them, and little six-year-old Keith was in boarding school. We all loaded into their Volkswagen van, the men in front and women and children in the back.

## Culture Shock Is More Than Surprise

As we left the airport my culture shock began. I had never seen anything like that in my life! I knew that I had a lot of adjusting to do. The roads were narrow, and people and animals walked on the road wherever they pleased. (One missionary, suffering from culture shock, said, "They can't walk down the road and stay out of the center.")

Missionaries commonly use the term "culture shock," but I really didn't understand what it meant for quite some time. I thought it was just being shocked at seeing different sights. However, culture shock is a condition or state of mind that a person gradually begins to live with. It slowly affects your nerves and emotions, until you react to people and situations uncharacteristically.

I think that most missionaries live in a state of culture shock during their first term on the mission field. That is why so many missionaries resign after their first term. If a missionary returns for a second term, they will find the work and place much more enjoyable.

It was interesting to see how differently the people were dressed. The women wore dresses with skirts made of many yards of white material that looked like cheesecloth. They wrapped a long, wide piece of material over their heads and around their shoulders. This was called a "*shama.*" Both the *shama* and the skirt had a wide colorful border that was woven into the material.

The men wore white trousers that looked like riding pants. They were tight up to the knees, then bloused at the thighs. They wore white shirts and jackets and also the *shama.*

I was embarrassed and shocked when I saw men relieving themselves along the sides of the road. But I had to realize that this was not America, and my whole concept of culture was in a retraining process.

The people lived in little mud huts with straw (thatched) roofs. Everything looked like mud and filth. I thought, "How can I ever live in this country?"

Our van seemed to be flying down the road as we constantly dodged people and animals. We went from one side to the other and down the middle as the horn blew continually. I was almost angry that Lonnie had let Bill drive so soon. I knew that we had to get used to the country, but this was ridiculous! We had just arrived, and he was not accustomed to driving in these conditions.

"Honey, be careful! Honey, watch out! Oh no, don't hit that donkey! Oh, honey, there's a man! Honey, please slow down." No one was paying much attention to my panic, except Georgine. I noticed that she looked at me rather strangely when I would yell a warning. "Well," I thought, "she is used to this zoo and I'm not."

We went by Bingham Academy, the boarding school where their small son, Keith, was living. When we stopped and got out of the van, I wanted to evaporate! Embarrassment is an understatement. I saw that the steering wheel was on the right side of the vehicle instead of the left! Bill was not driving, and I suddenly realized why I had gotten those strange looks from Georgine. I suppose I would also have looked strangely at some other woman who called my husband "honey" for five miles.

Wyvonna had been so good, but she was tired of being cooped up in planes and cars. Now she took the quick opportunity to run across the spacious lawn. As I called to her, little four-year-old Kelly ran to bring her back for me. Kelly was reaching for her when I yelled, "No Kelly, don't. . . ."

Too late! Wyvonna had already taken a bite out of her arm! That was a great way to develop a friendly relationship with our co-workers. Wyvonna was doing what she had learned to do before we left the States. Her cousin, Candy, was seven months older than she was and much bigger. Candy would pull her and pick her up, so Wyvonna quickly learned that her best defense was biting. I made the necessary apologies, tried to comfort Kelly, and soon the incident was behind us.

After we visited with Keith, we left and drove into the city of Addis Ababa. My neck and eyes were strained from trying to see everything at one time. I didn't want to miss a thing (except for the people who were still relieving themselves on the streets).

Lonnie parked near the post office (one of the most important places for the orientation of a new missionary). People gathered around the van before the men could get out. Vendors were trying to sell their wares. I learned my first Amharic word right there: *alfuligum*, which means, "I don't want." In the future I would use that term more than any other Amharic words.

The beggars were pushing their way to the vehicle with their hands out—men, women, and children with rags on their bodies. Many had gross physical deformities. They were dirty and stinking. I couldn't understand what they were saying.

"Oh, Lord. I want to go home. How can I ever live here and love these people?" I am sure that you have heard missionaries talk about loving the people before they ever go to the field. Pardon me, but I feel that statement comes from emotional hype. (I told you that I'm going to tell you the way it is—in my opinion.) Sometimes, after you live on the field, you wonder if you love them at all!

Young missionaries have confessed to me in agony, frustration, and guilt, "I don't think I even love these people."

That is a typical example of "culture shock."

One young missionary man came to us during a lot of stress. He put his head in his hands and said, "Oh, I hate these people." He didn't really hate them. He was suffering from the constant strain on the nerves of a foreign culture that had produced such a reaction. However, this very real feeling leads to guilt.

The devil wins many victories when he can keep us feeling guilty and unworthy. These are symptoms of culture shock. Most of it will pass with time, but young missionaries should be educated on this subject so they will not think that something unnatural is happening to them. In fact, venting and confessing your frustration actually helps (if you vent to the right people). It hurts us when we continually try to suppress the negative feelings; for fear that it is unspiritual. We must acknowledge the truth, pray for more grace and understanding, and it will eventually pass.

We laughed with the young man and said, "We all feel that way sometimes. You are experiencing normal culture shock."

At one time, we were living in a third-world country where we met a middle-aged couple while shopping one day. I heard them speaking English to each other and told Bill, "Those people are Americans."

We introduced ourselves to them and eventually became good friends. They were in their first term of mission work with another denomination. They had surrendered to missions after middle age, went to a very difficult field, and were in the stages of full-blown culture shock. They were releasing their stressful emotions on each other, and their marriage was in danger.

We explained to them that they were suffering from culture shock, not from being unspiritual or unworthy to be on the mission field. They were so relieved after our counsel, and they continued to do a good work on the field.

I think it is the love of God and obedience to Him, not love for the heathen people that you've never seen, that motivates a missionary to leave the comfort and safety of America. As the Bible says, "For the love of Christ constraineth us . . ." (2 Corinthians 5:14). Sure, we have a burden for them, want to take the Gospel, and see them saved from Hell. But we learn to love them later.

So, there. I have spoken my heart, and I am sure that many will disagree with me and think I am unspiritual. That's OK. I am being real. After all, I don't have to impress anyone except God (and our supporters!).

We left the post office and started to the apartment where we were to live while in language school. As we drove down the streets I did see some modern buildings, and along the sidewalks were six-foot tin fences. I learned that the fences were to hide the ugly mud huts that housed the typical Ethiopian people. Everything was so dirty. We laughed about the three-wheeled taxicabs that were all over the streets. Georgine told me, "You have a really nice apartment to live in. It is so much better than the tin house that we built in the country." I wasn't excited with the comparison. At the time, I didn't believe that anything was going to be "nice" in this place.

## My New Home

We drove down Haile Selassie Avenue, and soon Lonnie pointed to a tall, blue building on the right. "That is the mission building where you will live." He turned into the driveway and waited until an Ethiopian guard opened the gate to permit us to drive into the compound. We went down the driveway and parked in the small parking lot behind the building. Straight ahead was a stone wall, and on top of the wall was one of those high, tin fences, which separated the mission compound from the mud huts.

I looked to my right and on one side I saw a long, concrete building that housed the Ethiopian workers. On the other side was the back door to the four-story building that belonged to our mission.

On the ground floor was a chapel and training room, and missionary apartments were on the three upper floors. The large apartments housed the missionaries who were in language school, and the smaller ones were for the missionaries who were visiting Addis for business, supplies, etc. It was a nice building (for that country). In fact, the Communists later confiscated it and used it for their indoctrination center.

When we walked inside, my nose picked up the smell of the damp, cold, concrete building. I can still close my eyes and see and smell the aroma of that place. Mr. Able, our field director, informed us that our apartment was on the fourth floor. I was not really surprised at this point that there was no elevator! Remember that we had an infant, a toddler, and a baby due to be born in six months! The absence of an elevator remained a very real hardship during the following months of my pregnancy and the birth of our baby. (I *love* elevators.)

Our apartment consisted of a kitchen, living-dining room, two bedrooms, and a bath. Naturally, the walls were concrete, and the floors were hard tiles. It was not luxurious, but it was nice and very different than my visions of a tree house in the jungle. At least we had running water, an indoor bathroom, and the stairs were better than a ladder or grapevine.

The mission had provided temporary beds and household things for us to use until the arrival of our barrels and crates from the States. We shipped our beds, but we needed to buy furniture. (It would not be a very pleasant experience.)

I felt secure in the building since it was also home for Mr. and Mrs. Able and two other missionary families (friends from college.) We have many memories of the months that we lived in that building—happy and very unhappy ones.

# CHAPTER 9

## A New Culture

❧

After we had some time to rest and get over our jet lag, one of the other missionaries wanted to take us out to dinner. John had never had the reputation for being a conformist. He also had a great sense of humor, so I am sure that he needed a good laugh that night. He invited some of the other missionaries to go with us, and they took us to a typical Ethiopian restaurant.

As I walked in my eyes quickly scanned the place. I saw crude tables and chairs in a very plain, poorly lit little room. It certainly wasn't high-class, but I was a missionary now and I could handle it.

We all sat down at a long table and ordered the traditional food—*injerra* and *wat*—, which I was eager to try. We were having a great time with these old friends when the food came.

The Ethiopian waiter sat my food in front of me. I didn't examine it closely for fear of what I might find. (On the mission field, you eat and don't look or ask questions—at least that is what the older missionaries try to teach you.)

The *wat* was similar to a thick stew with meat and potatoes and was highly seasoned. They told me that the *injerra* was bread, but it looked like a large pancake that was cooked on one side. I could see the bubbled effect in it, like a pancake that has not been turned. They cut it in strips to serve it that night for the foreigners. The missionaries instructed us to tear off a piece of the *injerra*, wrap it around some of the *wat*, and pick it up—without using a fork. No problem!

I thought if I could go to Africa, I could eat their food. I tore off a piece of *injerra* about two inches long, picked up some *wat*, and started to my mouth. My fingers were covered in the juice, and the *injerra* felt like a thin, damp sponge in my hand. I made the forbidden mistake of looking at it before I put it in my mouth.

What is that? Hair in my *wat*? Oh, boy! I feared something like this. Remember my weak stomach? I quietly laid it aside, prayed for a strong stomach, and was willing to overlook it. After all, I reasoned, a hair could get in any cook's food.

I made my second attempt. Naturally, this time I couldn't keep from looking—bad decision! Some of the meat in my *wat* was covered with hair! Now, even though I have an awfully weak stomach, I have an equally strong determination. I tried the third time—same thing. I didn't say anything, but just sat quietly. It wasn't long until John noticed that I wasn't eating.

"LaMoin, you're not eating. Don't you like the food? It will offend them if you don't eat it."

"John, I've never eaten hair in the States, and I'm not going to eat hair in Ethiopia."

This provided a great laugh for everyone. I wasn't laughing. It seemed that the cook had not properly skinned the goat before cooking it, and I drew the lucky dish. The other food was OK. I still believe John set me up. It took a long time, but I finally learned to like *injerra* and *wat*.

## New Furniture

With the settling-in process, we had to furnish our apartment. It was not possible to go to a nice furniture store and choose pretty, comfortable things. We went to a little side street that was called "furniture row." There were little crude shacks on either side of the dirt road. We trudged through mud and the smell of urine, until we came to a little shop where they were making furniture.

The saws were humming and sawdust was flying as we followed the man through the mire to look at the finished products. We were looking for a sofa set. The few sets were setting out in the open, collecting sawdust. There was no clean, pretty showroom to display the furniture.

We finally selected a dark green set that included a sofa, chair, footstool, and coffee table. The sofa and chair had wooden legs and arms. The seats were hard—stuffed with straw—and very uncomfortable.

We also purchased a table and six chairs and had them delivered. No, there was no delivery van. A man put the table upside down on his head, balanced a chair on each of the table legs with the other two on top of the table, and carried them to our house. (This was the typical way to carry things in Africa. I tried it once in America by putting a mattress on my head to carry it. I almost broke my neck; it was sore for weeks.) Bill made a buffet for the dining room. We bought a very small refrigerator and cookstove. I bought some local cloth and made curtains for all the windows. We were even able to get a rug to put in the living room. Our house was beginning to look like a home, but not like an American home.

## My First Experience in Ethiopian Food Stores

Next I had to learn how to shop for food, and Gail offered to help me. She had been in Ethiopia for six months and had learned her way around quite well. She explained to me that there were about five small shops where we could buy our staples, such as flour, sugar, oil, etc. It was important to compare prices, because many times an item was quite a bit cheaper at one of the shops than at the others.

These shops were certainly not like Kroger's back home. We walked into the front door and faced a counter that extended across the width of the small shop. All of the food items were on shelves behind the counter, and we had to ask the shopkeeper for each item. It was a little like the old general store in western movies. It was a very slow process.

The items were not numerous, so it didn't take as long to make decisions as it does in the large supermarkets in the States. If we could find what we needed, there was only one brand, so choices were few.

After we selected what we wanted, the shopkeeper wrote each item and price on a piece of paper, totaled the cost, and we paid him. This was very archaic, but we were in the middle of Africa and felt blessed to even have the limited products. I just hated having to go to all of the shops to find what I needed, but we had to live as economically as possible.

Gail took me to the bread shop. As she was making her selections I was surveying the open bins of unwrapped bread. Various bugs and flies were eating their portion before it could be removed while all kinds of human hands were feeling it to check for freshness. It didn't take me long to decide what I wanted!

Gail bought her bread and then turned to me. "This is really pretty good bread. How much do you want?"

"None. I'm not about to eat that dirty bread. You don't know how many germs are on that stuff."

She laughed, "Yeah, I know it's not like at home, but you'll get used to it. This is the only kind we can get so you have to use it." Wrong! I never got used to it. I started baking my own bread. I later taught my housegirl to make the most beautiful and delicious loaves of yeast bread in Ethiopia.

The meat market was another challenge. I could smell it before we got to it. The meat was hung in slabs in the open air—no refrigeration! The flies had also beaten us to the meat. I knew that my ingenuity was limited, and I had no choice but to buy the meat, unless I decided to be a vegetarian (which would not have been difficult). I had to learn what part of the slab to ask for, and we ordered it by the kilo, which is a little over two pounds. We would tell the butcher what we wanted; he would shoo the flies away and whack it off with a very sharp knife.

Because the meat was so tough, we had to use a pressure cooker for most of it. This did more than tenderize it, it also was sure to kill any worms that might be in the meat. Tapeworm is very prominent in Africa, so we had to be very careful that we didn't eat any rare meat. If we ordered in a restaurant, we would say, "Please burn a steak and bring it to me." I still won't eat rare meat.

Next was the vegetable market. We went to an open-air market and waded in mud, rotten vegetables, urine, and various other things as we haggled over the price of each kilo of vegetables.

The fruit and vegetables were dirty and could be sure to contain various germs that could be very dangerous to the health. Immediately upon entering the house with them I put them in strong bleach water and soaked them for twenty minutes to kill the germs. Then I rinsed them with cooled, boiled water and stored them in the refrigerator. Shopping for food was a pain in the foot and took a whole day. Can you understand why I still hate to shop for groceries, even in the States? I put it off until the last minute.

We had been in the country a couple of weeks, and we were hungry for good Southern fried chicken. I went to the meat market with a mental picture of fried chicken, mashed potatoes, gravy, and good, homemade biscuits. I was glad that I could at least buy the chicken and not have to kill it, as my mother did when I was a child.

Mother raised chickens when we lived in the country. She would go out, catch a couple of nice fryers, take the head in her hand, give the chicken a good sharp twist, and the head would separate from the body. She would quickly cover the chickens with a big galvanized washtub, so they would not flop on the ground and get dirty and bruised.

She didn't want the chickens "running around with their heads off."

I had watched her kill chickens so many times, and it looked so easy. One day, when I was about twelve years of age, we were going to have fried chicken for dinner.

"Mother, let me kill the chickens."

"Do you think you can?" she asked.

"Sure."

She helped me catch one; I gave the neck a good twist but nothing happened. I am pretty persistent, and I wasn't going to be beaten by a chicken, so I tried again. I continued to swing that chicken around and around, but I could never break its neck. Mother finally grew tired of seeing the abuse, took it from me, and with one quick twist, the poor chicken was out of its misery. I never wanted to kill another chicken.

Now there I stood in an open, smelly, repulsive, African meat market to buy a chicken. The chickens were not neatly wrapped in clear paper with a government-approved sticker on them. Instead, these chickens were plucked bare-naked with their heads and feet still attached. (I have just now realized that I don't know how they killed those poor birds!)

They looked gross, but I was now a missionary, and I could handle the challenge. I bought one, took it home, cut off the head and feet, and proceeded to cut it up (I had successfully learned this from my mother). I floured and fried it and prepared all the other food to make a great Southern meal.

Bill was enthusiastically waiting to dig into this delicious, familiar food. We asked God to bless it and served our plates. We took a big bite of that fried chicken and began to chew, and chew, and chew, and . . . I later put it in the pressure cooker! That chicken was destined to be eaten, tough or not.

Later, the Africans taught me how to select a tender chicken. The trick is to put a finger on each side of the breastbone and put your thumb in the middle to feel the end of the bone. If it is flexible, the chicken is young and tender; if not, don't buy it. Alertness is still required. Many times the butchers would break the breastbone so it would be flexible. Oh, the lessons I learned on the mission field!

# CHAPTER 10

## *Necessary Evils*

***K***eeping house and cooking was a full time job. I had to be so careful with everything in the house, and especially in the kitchen, because of so many germs and diseases in the country.

All of our water had to be boiled for at least twenty minutes. I always had a pot of water boiling and some cooling. I kept containers filled with boiled water in the kitchen for cooking and in the bathroom for brushing our teeth. Some of the missionaries laughed at me because they brushed their teeth with the water. It seemed to make sense to me that if the germs got into my mouth, they could get down my throat. Anyway, I didn't want to risk letting my family get sick like others who had suffered with Hepatitis and other illnesses.

I made sure that my floors were cleaned every day with a strong disinfectant. We could bring in any disease on our feet, and I had small children playing on the floors.

All of the cooking was done from "scratch." Preparation of a meal took a long time. Everything took a long time.

## Language School Didn't Help

Bill and I had to start to language school a few weeks after arriving in Ethiopia. Wyvonna was not accustomed to being with an Ethiopian babysitter who spoke very little English. It was so hard to leave her in the morning to go to class. I could hear her screaming as we walked down the four flights of stairs and out the front door. It was not conducive to studying the language.

I hated the language study anyway. I think it was because of having to leave the girls. I couldn't concentrate, and I was uncomfortable (I was about five months pregnant). The language was hard, and I just didn't have a desire to study it. (I told you that I am going to be truthful in this book. Maybe it will be a comfort to some other missionary who is feeling the same way I felt.)

I know that the experts recommend studying the language as soon as possible after arriving in a foreign country. However, I feel that it is better to wait until you feel somewhat comfortable with the environment, people, cooking, and lifestyle. It is a large adjustment to get used to living in a third-world country and to have to study language in the process is too much strain (in my opinion).

One day, when I was suffering with a good case of bad attitude, one of the missionaries came to visit. She happened to be one of those who acted more spiritual than I did. I was expressing some of my frustration in trying to learn the language. She must have thought I was a hopeless case. I was just being honest and permitting my inner feelings to show. You must be very careful who sees inside your heart if you don't want to be criticized. Of course, it didn't matter very much to me at that time.

She said, "Don't you want to learn the language?"

I replied, "I don't care if I learn it or not." (That wasn't true.)

Amharic has feminine and masculine gender. She used the words for boy and girl and asked, "Don't you want to know if your daughters are *blank* (boys) or *blank* (girls)?" (I don't remember the Amharic words.)

I looked at her and wondered when she would finally get caught in the net and be dressed in the white coat with sleeves that tie in the back.

Occasionally, there would be an amusing thing about language school that I enjoyed. Each day we had to go outside with our own individual Ethiopian "informant" (even the term isn't comfortable to me). It was supposed to give us the opportunity to visit, talk, and practice the language that we were trying to learn. We were required to speak to each other in Amharic. However, I cheated a lot.

The sun was shining beautifully one day, and it was very warm when my instructor said, "Oh, let's move under this tree."

"Why? I like it in the sun."

"But it will make me black." (I think you are astute enough to understand my surprise.)

A few months after I had dropped out of school, I was shopping when I happened to meet my former language teacher who was an American.

"Are you still studying the language?" he asked.

"I am learning from my housegirl."

"But you won't learn the proper Amharic from her."

I was thinking, "What difference does it make? All I want to do is to be able to speak in the language. I'm not planning to write an Amharic book or teach a class." That was stupid and ignorant mentality on my part because now I realize he was correct. However, at that time I was young and trying to adjust to a very difficult country and culture.

## Housegirls Didn't Help My Attitude

To add to the confusion, it was a necessity to have someone to help with the house and with the children. The wages were very cheap for people to work in the house, and all of the missionaries used the Ethiopians to help them. This also helped to provide work for them, and they helped to teach us the language and customs.

Yeshi came to me highly recommended by a missionary from another mission. She was very pleasant, reasonably clean, and spoke a little English, so I hired her. She was good with the children and had been trained to do a little cooking.

Soon after Yeshi came to work for me, I purchased eggs and put them in the refrigerator. One day I came home, started to cook dinner, and couldn't find my eggs.

"Yeshi, where are the eggs?" I asked.

"I make custard." She beamed.

In her desire to please us, she had made custard and used a dozen eggs! I was patient and controlled my temptation to strangle her. However, I almost lost it when I discovered that she had put cinnamon in the gravy!

Since I was pregnant and didn't have a washing machine, Yeshi was a blessing when it came to doing the laundry—with exceptions, of course!

We arrived in Ethiopia in the winter, and it was damp and cold. Wyvonna didn't have enough warm clothing, so, with much difficulty, I was able to find a little pair of brown pants made of heavy flannel. They were real cute, and they kept her warm. When I came home one day, she was wearing them. I took a second look. I was seeing spots before my eyes, but I wasn't sick. I realized quickly that Yeshi didn't know how to use bleach when she did the washing! I was so upset about those pants. It was so hard to find *anything* decent to buy in Ethiopia, and when we did, it was expensive. Now she had ruined Wyvonna's pants. I realized that it was really my fault for giving her the bleach, so she escaped unharmed!

Yeshi was very good, loved the children, and tried hard to please. We had a good working relationship. One day she came and asked to have a week off. Someone in her family was very ill, and she had to take care of them. This was a very real inconvenience for me, but I gave her permission to go. I could hardly wait until she came back. I really missed all the work that she did, plus helping with the children.

After a week, she returned. She worked one day and asked me if she could have a week off to prepare for her brother's wedding. I quickly examined my body but didn't see a sign that said, "I'm stupid." I almost came unglued. By this time I was about eight months pregnant, tired, and suffering from culture shock!

"Sure, you can have the week off, and don't bother to come back," I told her as I almost breathed fire on her.

"But, madam, it's custom for me to prepare for my brother's wedding."

"Fine, go prepare for it, but don't come back."

I didn't pray about my decision before I fired her. I realize that I was very unspiritual and quick to wrath, but at least I didn't follow through on my temptation to kick her down the stairs! She had stepped on my last nerve!

I lived to regret firing Yeshi. (We usually do regret snap decisions.) Not having to do all the housework and not having the full responsibility of the children had spoiled me.

A couple of weeks after I fired her, I was down in the laundry room on the ground floor. As I stated earlier, I didn't have a washing machine. We did the laundry in large concrete tubs that had ridged surfaces on one side to scrub the clothes. It was similar to our old-fashioned washboards, which my mother used when I was a child.

Get the picture: Here I was, eight months pregnant. After carrying the clothes down four flights of stairs, I was scrubbing Bill's khaki pants and shirts, sheets, towels, etc. in that old concrete washtub with my hands. I was not singing *Count Your Many Blessings* at that point, and I would have seriously injured the first person to say, "You'll get your rewards in Heaven." I was having a good pity party!

While I was in the height of my discontent, mental murmuring, and complaining, Yeshi walked in the door. She was a little hesitant about approaching me. I had succeeded in "getting my bluff in on her." No Ethiopian houseworker was going to get the best of me. Yeshi had been blessed all these past months anyway. I always had a second girl to help with the cleaning. Yeshi had taken care of the children and helped in the kitchen.

Now, I didn't acquire the title of "LaMoin's Employment Agency" for no reason. I had hired and fired more workers than I could remember. They were impossible! Dumb! (They were dumb to our culture and methods, but not in their own ways.) That's why we called them "necessary evils." We needed them, but they could drive you around the bend.

Don't be quick to criticize me. Go live in Ethiopia for a while, and then you can judge me. They were really like children. They didn't know any better. But remember I was adjusting to a new and strange country. It had taken its toll, and I was reacting.

I was not the only missionary that had problems with my house help. One of the other missionaries in the building had a boy working for her. She was really mad at him one day because she thought he had been rude to her friend who was visiting. She was in the middle of her scolding, really giving him the one, two.

"I don't ever want you to be rude to anyone in this house again. I will fire you, (etc., etc., etc.). Do you understand 'rude'?" (He spoke English.)

"Oh, yes, madam. That's what holds a tree in the ground."

I felt like hugging and kissing Yeshi, but I maintained my employer attitude. If I had let her know that I had missed her and couldn't do the work myself, she would surely take advantage of me later. I had not fallen off a turnip truck!

She spoke. I spoke—very coldly. She asked for her job back. She was sorry, and she really wanted to come back to work for me. I hummed, hawed, and pretended that I didn't know if I wanted her to work for me again. Poor thing! I had her begging for the job, and finally I gave in! I warned her about what I expected in the future, and then it didn't take long for me to rip my apron off, put it on her, and we lived happily ever after, until we left Ethiopia!

## Yeshi Was a Treasure

She was the best worker that I ever found. The whole family loved her and she loved us. The kids adored her.

When we left Ethiopia, she walked to the plane with us crying and saying, "Oh, my babies. You are taking them so far away."

Yeshi came to work one morning and was crying. I asked her to come and sit with me in the living room. "What's wrong, Yeshi? Did someone die?" I asked.

"No, madam. My mother-in-law is driving me crazy." After talking to her for awhile, I told her that we have in-law problems also, and she calmed down and started to laugh.

She came to work very upset another day. Upon inquiring about the problem, I was told that she was wearing her new dress so she could show it to me. When she got off the bus, she caught part of the full skirt on something sharp and ripped it. It took a long time for her to save the money to buy the new dress, and now she was heartbroken because she thought it was ruined. Being a normal, emotional woman, she was crying her heart out. I almost cried for her and felt so sorry for her—my friend.

I calmed her down and told her that I would repair the dress. I immediately got my needle and thread and was extra careful with my tiny stitches. When I finished, she was elated because the damage could not be seen.

Yeshi asked us to visit her home, and we happily agreed. Bill and I dressed in our Ethiopian clothes for the occasion. We drove through the dirt streets and impoverished African neighborhoods, until we came to her home.

Her one-room, mud house was in a compound with several other houses of the same type. She was all smiles as she invited us into her home. She happily showed us different things and seemed so pleased that her home was better than most of the other mud houses.

She took pride in her papered walls of old newspapers and magazines. She was especially proud of the American magazines with pictures. Her walls were covered with these treasures. She had a small square table and three chairs. Her cooking utensils sat on the floor in one corner. She even had a proper bed. (A lot of the Ethiopians have only animal skins that are rolled out on the floor at night to serve as their beds.)

There was a communal kitchen with an open fire where they cooked their *injerra*. She demonstrated the techniques of making *injerra* and asked me if I would like to try. I was happy to have a go at it.

She handed me a large tin can with sour-smelling batter made of a wheat mixture that had fermented for a few days. I poured the batter onto an open, black surface in a clockwise fashion, starting at the outside and going to the center. We watched as the batter ran together and cooked until the bubbles appeared; then she removed it. We ate it later in her home.

Her kitchen containers were not glass or nice plastic but tin cans that the missionaries had thrown away. She had a few dishes that missionaries had given to her. She was considered to be upper class by her neighbors. Because she worked for Americans, she could even pay her own housegirl to keep her son and to clean for her.

She felt honored to have us in her home. She introduced us to her neighbors and proudly made us acquainted with her small son and her husband.

She also let me have a try at pulverizing the hot red peppers that were an essential ingredient in the *wat*. She led me to a hollow tree stump, where she placed the peppers. Then she handed me a large, round pole that I had to use both hands to hold. I was instructed to pound on the peppers in an up and down motion with the pole, until they were ground to powder.

Our visit was very enjoyable and informative. Getting an insight into how these dear people lived made me even more thankful for the abundant blessings and wealth that we have as Americans.

# CHAPTER 11

# I Had to Learn to Keep Laughing

Addis Ababa (which means "new flower") was a large, semi-modern city. Ethiopia was one of the few countries in Africa that was not colonized by the British, but the Italians took control during the war. In spite of their cruelty during the occupation of Mussolini's army, they had done much to improve the general lifestyle in Ethiopia.

They built roads throughout the country which made it possible to transport supplies. The roads through the mountains were a work of fine engineering. Ethiopia was called the Switzerland of Africa. We have seen snow through some of those extremely high mountains. Without roads, they would have been isolated.

There were many Italians, Armenians, and Greeks who lived in Addis. They ran the little shops and businesses.

There were a few stores where we could buy some of the necessities, but we had to ship most of our needed supplies from the States. We packed and shipped about fifty large, steel fifty-five-gallon drums. We felt like Ala Baba and the forty thieves. We took everything we felt we needed to live and to serve the Lord in that primitive country.

## One of My Moments of Stupidity

There were many thieves on the streets, so we had to be very alert when we went to town. Soon after we arrived, we parked our van in front of the shop we had to visit, and I made the stupid mistake of leaving my purse in the car. I thought it would be OK since I could watch it from the window while Bill was buying what he needed.

I know you are thinking, "She should have known better than that." I know it was dumb, but it was in one of my weaker moments. I just didn't want to carry that heavy purse. A policeman was standing in front of the vehicle, so I thought it must be safe. (Well, I had to learn, didn't I?)

I watched the van while Bill made his purchase. We walked out and opened the door of the van to get in. My heart skipped a couple of beats! Of course, the purse was gone! They had gotten it when I turned my back to walk into the shop. The policeman had not seen a thing. (Sure!)

I have *never* made that mistake again. That lesson has stayed with me the rest of my life. I still panic if I think I have lost my purse. Missionaries learn many practical lessons on the field that last a lifetime.

One day I was shopping in the States, when suddenly, I almost panicked. "Where's my purse?" It was on my arm! I can always spot a female missionary anywhere in the world by the way she carries her purse. One of our missionaries was in Addis by herself when a young man grabbed her purse and ran. She ran after him, tackled him on the sidewalk, and retrieved her treasure.

## Shaleen's Eye Was Swollen Shut

Because of the poor sanitary conditions and the ignorance of the people, disease was rampant. The urination on the streets drew thousands of flies that would then spread the diseases everywhere. It was a common sight to see children with pus-filled eyes, covered with flies.

Once we were returning from a trip to one of the northern mission stations when I noticed pus collecting in one of Shaleen's eyes. She was only about one year old. I held her and tried to keep the pus wiped from her eyes during the four-hour ride back to Addis. By the time we arrived home, both of her eyes were infected, almost swollen shut, and the pus continued to drain from her little eyes.

We immediately took her to a doctor. After using the medicine he gave us to put in her eyes, she healed quickly. The flies spread this type of infection, and if it isn't treated, eventually the eyelashes will turn inside and rub against the eyeball. The condition causes blindness and will destroy the eye like a cancer.

## Disease Was Everywhere

Lepers freely walked the streets, begging, for their existence. Sometimes, they threatened to touch those who did not give them money. The government provided leper colonies, but the conditions were not good, and since they were not compulsive, most lepers preferred their freedom to live by begging.

I have seen people, sitting on the sidewalk in downtown Addis, whose feet and legs were swollen to many times their normal size, due to Elephantiasis. The skin would be thick and rough, with the appearance of elephant skin. The toes and feet were cracked open. These people would sit on the streets because they were in the final stages of the disease and could no longer walk. Elephantiasis is a blood parasite that is fatal without proper treatment.

Bill was sitting in the car at the post office when a beggar approached him. He refused to give him money, so he suddenly pulled back his *shama* and exposed his throat that was eaten away. His tongue was visible through the hole. He then threatened to touch Bill if he didn't give him money.

People in the Western world get the wrong idea when missionaries talk about refusing to give money to the beggars. I suppose that we can become too hardened to the needs, but when you live in a country where there are thousands of people who survive by begging, your senses become dulled to it. We could never give to all the beggars, and when we gave to one, there would immediately be a crowd of them surrounding us. They became very angry if you gave to one and not to all of them.

Jesus said that we would always have the poor with us, and we did not have the resources to supply their physical needs. They were too great and unending. It was indeed heartbreaking to see little children by the hundreds, who were ragged and hungry, begging for money on the streets. Many of them were professionals who had been trained by their parents to beg. Sometimes, the parents would even cripple the children when they were babies and raise them to beg. Some actually prospered by this method, while others simply survived.

Bill was inside a store, and I was waiting in the car with Wyvonna (who was about two years old). She had partially eaten a piece of cake, grew tired of it, and threw the rest out of the window. A little boy about six years old quickly grabbed it from the dirty, germ-infested ground. As he was eating it he happily exclaimed, "This is good!" These heartbreaking experiences were a part of everyday life.

Our Western eyes were shocked and our hearts were broken as we saw grown men fighting over a garbage can. Soon, because of the struggle, the can turned over, and the rotten contents spilled out on the puddles of filthy, sewage water on the street. We watched as they pushed and shoved to pick up the food, which had fallen to the ground. Every American is rich by these standards, and we should daily thank God that we were born in America.

The people were thrilled over a well-worn garment that was given to them, things that we would throw in the trash. We saw a man coming down the street, walking with an air of royalty. His head was high and his steps quick and confident. We looked him up and down and saw that he wore nice rubber boots, but, to our surprise, they had no feet—just the tops. He was happy and felt proud of those footless boots.

There was a creek a few blocks from our apartment building where people could be seen bathing, washing clothes, and drawing water for cooking. One day we saw a man going to the creek wearing only a towel on his shoulder! This was in the middle of Addis Ababa. (And we missionaries had been instructed not to wear sleeveless dresses!)

No one could have convinced me earlier that I would become so accustomed to these sights that I would take them for granted, but gradually that happened.

We had to maintain a sense of humor, or the poverty and culture shock would have made us candidates for a home for the bewildered. We tried to find the humor, even in the suffering.

## Bill Shouldn't Have Sent Me to the Bank

Bill and some of the other missionaries were working on the church, so he asked me to go downtown and cash a check. He usually took care of all the business, so this was a new experience for me.

We lived only a few blocks from our bank, so I decided to waddle down there (I was pregnant). On the way, I passed a couple of smaller banks before I arrived at the large bank where we had our account. As I approached the door I noticed the soldier who was guarding the bank. He stood nonchalantly scratching his chin with the barrel of his submachine gun. I hurried past him and prayed that it wouldn't go off.

I walked into the bank, wrote out the check, and went to the cashier who handled the foreign accounts. He looked at it, asked me several questions about my account (trying to impress me with his knowledge), and then refused to cash it.

We always deposited our American checks in the bank, and our mission had a letter of security on file that guaranteed the checks. This had never happened before. I couldn't understand it. I tried in vain to convince him that the check was good. Finally, my reasoning was getting close to anger, so I asked to see the president of the bank. I believe if you want to accomplish something, go to the top!

After I explained everything to the president, he also refused to cash the check. (They really did not like to do business with a woman.) Finally, I lost my control and gave him a piece of my mind!

"Well, if this is the way you're going to treat me, I'll just take my business to another bank!"

With that announcement, I whirled around and proudly marched out of the bank. I was so angry. How dare he treat me like that! Didn't he realize that I was an American! (Big deal!) I fumed back to where the men were working and triumphantly related the incident to them.

Our good friend, Delmar Powell, who had been in Ethiopia for about two years, laughed so hard he couldn't speak. Well, I was not sharing the humor at this point.

"What's so funny, Del?" I angrily asked.

Trying to regain his composure, he finally was able to say during his laughing, "LaMoin, don't you know that's the *only* bank in Ethiopia?'

"Well, what about the other ones that I saw on the way there?"

"Those are only branches. That is the government-owned Bank of Ethiopia, and there is no other."

I was comforted by the fact that I left that bank president scratching his head and wondering if another one had been opened. After all these years, every time I see Delmar, he laughs and asks me about my banking business.

Bill went into the same bank to cash a check, and the teller gave him a hard time. I think our balance was seven hundred dollars. The teller, in his attempt to show his importance, said, "Let me see the balance in your checkbook."

"Sure," Bill said. "No problem." He quickly added three zeros behind the balance figure and handed it to the teller. His eyes grew large when he arrogantly examined it and saw $700,000.00.

"Oh, that is very good!" he remarked as he quickly handed the money to Bill.

## Don't Tell Us That We Can't Eat Here

We were fortunate to have a few nice restaurants that provided good food and a break from the routine. These were designed for the tourists, to try to give a favorable impression of the country.

Bill and I had been on a trip up country with John and Gail. We arrived back in Addis after dark. We were dirty, tired, and hungry. When I say dirty, I mean that we were covered with so much dust from the dirt roads that my black hair looked blond.

We went to the Ghion Hotel, which had a very nice dining room, even a violinist! We walked into the front door and asked for a table. The waiter looked us up and down and informed us, in a very cool tone, that we could not come in because we were not dressed appropriately.

John has never accepted a no in his life. He pulled a large roll of one-dollar bills from his pocket as he sternly retorted, "Where's the owner? I'll just buy this place, and you will be the first to lose your job."

The waiter's eyes almost popped out as he caught a glimpse of the large roll of money and quickly said, "Oh, that's quite all right, sir. Please follow me." He led us to the best table in the dining room.

Laughter can flatten out problems, and everyday life in Ethiopia provided much humor. We just had to see it through the fog of culture shock. The Bible says "A merry heart doeth good like a medicine . . ." (Proverbs 17:22). I am convinced that laughter is not only therapeutic, it can save your sanity on the mission field! If a missionary takes nothing else in his suitcase, he'd better pack his sense of humor. It is essential equipment.

One day there was a knock at our door, and I opened it. One of the workers asked me if I had seen Gabriel, another worker. We were new in the country, and I didn't know Gabriel.

"I don't know him. What does he look like?" I asked. (Dumb question to start.)

"Oh, he's the black one."

They all looked black to me, having recently arrived in Africa! I had not yet learned to distinguish between the tones. For example, the people from Sudan are *very* black, and the Ethiopians are brown-toned.

## Head Lice Was Also a Problem

My friend, Georgine, came to visit me one day with her two little girls. Kelly and Karen had very long, thick hair. Karen was sitting on the floor, between Georgine's legs. While we talked I was puzzled about what Georgine was doing. She would take a strand of Karen's hair between her fingernails and pull it from the roots to the ends. At first I thought it was a nervous habit, but my curiosity finally triumphed.

"Georgine, what are you doing to her hair?"

"Pulling out the nits."

"What are nits?"

She acted surprised, as if everyone knew what nits were.

"The girls have head lice, and nits are the eggs from the lice."

"Head lice?"

"Oh, yes, most of the children have them. We have tried everything to get rid of them. They just don't have the right kind of medicine here to kill them. I am having some sent from the States."

By this time, I was almost in a state of cardiac arrest! My children had been playing with these girls. Lice! I had always heard about lice but had never had them or seen anyone with them. I remembered hearing my mother say that the only way you could get rid of them was to shave the head. I looked at my pretty little daughters and saw bald heads. Thank God, they never had lice the whole time we were in Africa.

A few years later, I remember visiting some missionaries in the Philippines. One of the ladies had a cute little girl, about a year old. I took her on my lap and was playing with her when her mother casually mentioned that she had been trying to get rid of the child's head lice. I almost threw the child across the room. I'm not joking. That was my first impulse. I have a very strong aversion to head lice.

## Fleas Lived on People

Soon after our arrival, we were visiting with Denton, another missionary friend who lived in the building. I noticed red spots all over his face, neck, and arms.

"Do you have a rash?" I asked. He looked surprised as he started examining himself.

"Oh, no. Those are flea bites."

"Sure," I smirked. (Go ahead and have your fun with the new kid on the block.)

"I'm not kidding. We all get them here. You'll see."

It didn't take me long to realize that he was telling me the truth. Fleas were everywhere. Shaleen was a baby, and she got bites while sleeping in her crib. She looked like she had the measles.

Bill came home from the first service in his newly started church, and I didn't let him come into the house until he was "de-fleaed." He was wearing light Khaki clothing, and I could see the fleas jumping all over him.

Our African guard carried a baboon on his shoulder, and the monkey was constantly picking fleas from the guard's head and clothing. Of course, that was food for the baboon, so it served a dual purpose.

We would go to bed at night and feel them crawling on our legs. We soon worked out a "killer" system. We had a light switch on a cord at our bed. I would turn out the light and keep the push button switch in my hand. Bill would take hold of the bed covers, and we would wait quietly, not moving. It didn't take long for one of us to feel a flea crawling on our legs.

Bill (or I—whoever was the intended dinner) would whisper, "I feel one." At the same time I would switch on the light, Bill would throw off the covers and press the flea with his thumb. After he broke his legs and made him unconscious (well, use your imagination), he would crush him between his thumbnails. That was a nightly routine.

We also sprinkled DDT powder onto our mattresses and patted it into the bed. We have been told since then that the powder was very dangerous, but so were the fleas! I would rather take my chances with the DDT—it didn't itch.

One of our friends was having some medical problems, and she had to return to the States for some treatment. She was asked to give a testimony in a church, so she was telling about some of the funny things in Ethiopia. She proceeded to tell them about the fleas and other pests, and in her excitement, her mouth ran ahead of her brain, and she ended by saying, "Why, I have learned to just sleep with any old thing." Her face was red as the people roared in laughter.

## "Split Flea" Soup

The fleas were a real problem. Our mission director came from the States to visit all of us. We were having a special evening out with him. We went to the Ethiopian Hotel where they had a nice restaurant. Our first course was split pea soup. Everyone was eating, laughing, and talking, but I happened to be looking at my soup (some of us are just slow learners).

"Is that pepper in there?" I was thinking to myself.

Upon a closer examination, I saw that it was fleas! In our soup! I alerted the rest of the party, but for some it was too late; they had already eaten most of their soup. After all these years, we still laugh about our "split flea" soup.

## No Fish, Thank You

John and Bill went fishing in an old, extinct volcano that some missionaries had stocked with catfish many years before. They caught a few, and Bill brought two of them up to our apartment to show them to me. Then he had to decide what to do with them. He decided to just put them in the bathtub and to tell Yeshi to clean them.

He told her to go into the bathroom and clean the fish. She obeyed, and, suddenly, we heard her screaming. We ran to the bathroom and learned that when she started to pick up the fish thinking it was dead, the fish flopped and nearly scared her white. She refused to touch them again, so Bill ended up cleaning them. Later, I refused to cook them.

John asked us to come to their place and eat fish the next evening. Gail had cooked cornbread and fried the fish, and they were so good. After we finished eating, I asked her how she prepared them. To my utter horror, they explained to me that you have to soak the fish in cold water overnight so the worms will crawl out of the flesh. I don't vomit easily, but if I could have that night, I would have given their fish back to them—right in the living room.

We learned that the fish were "mud-catfish." They were scavengers and unfit to eat (in my opinion). I threw ours away. I like fish, but not that much. It is hard for me to eat catfish today. When I order them in a restaurant, I always ask if they are "pond-grown." I hope people haven't lied to me, but I have been told that they are good to eat.

## Our Cockeyed Dentist

Bill had a tooth that was bothering him, so we went to the only dentist in town. I think he was an Italian. I don't really remember, but he was comical. We weren't impressed at first sight of him. Bless his heart, his eyes weren't straight. When he talked to us, one eye looked at us and the other looked way off to the side. He used a pencil that was so big around that he could hardly hold it.

He asked me to get into the dental chair. I explained that I didn't have a problem, but Bill did. He insisted on checking my teeth first. He was raving on about what good teeth I had as he held both of his hands in front of him and tapped his fingers together. He told Bill, "Pearls. Absolute pearls. You are a very lucky man." (Why? They were my teeth.)

He put Bill in the chair and almost had his head in Bill's mouth while he examined him. Then he called me over to show me his teeth. He was stretching his lips extra wide so both of us could view the problem. He finally pronounced his diagnosis, but by that time, Bill had changed his mind about having the tooth fixed.

Soon after that, Richard, a missionary on a country station, came to our house. He had an abscessed tooth that was causing a lot of pain. We told him about this dentist, and he decided to give him a try, even though we weren't very optimistic.

When he returned from the dentist, his mouth was still numb. The dentist had removed his molar, and he felt temporarily relieved. However, when the feeling started returning, he painfully discovered that the dentist had extracted the wrong tooth!

Richard went back and told him that he had removed a good tooth and that the bad one was still hurting. The dentist looked at his teeth again. He finally said, "That one is very bad. You'd better wait until you go back to the States to have that one removed." (And the dentist still lived.) Richard moaned for a few days. Finally, the Lord had compassion on him and took away the pain.

Poor Richard had his share of problems. He lived on a desert mission station where the *Idals* (desert people) frequently ran their cattle and goats across his property. He finally saved enough money to put a fence around the property, to keep the cattle from ruining his garden and yard. However, that didn't stop them. They broke down his fence several times. He was pretty tired of the *Idals* and their animals by this time.

One day, they ran their goats into his yard. He tied two of them to a tree and went into the village to get the police, to show them what he had to endure. When they returned, in line with his luck, he found that one goat had kicked the other goat to death. Then he was accused of being the cause of the loss of the goat. To make matters worse, the dead goat was pregnant; so that meant he had deprived the *Idals* of two goats. With God's help, he finally managed to get out of that trying dilemma.

## Snake Stories

Our only source of good meat was the fresh game that the men killed. The forests were full of deer, wild boar, and other good animals and birds.

Richard went hunting one day with some of his Ethiopian workers. He wasn't feeling well that day, and soon he became tired. He saw a big log and sat down on it to rest. His workers became panicky and were yelling, "Snake, snake."

Richard quickly responded, "Where, where?"

"You're sitting on it."

Richard had very bad eyesight. He saw the body of the huge snake, but the rest of it was covered by bush. It had rough texture and, with his poor eyesight, it looked like a log. He quickly made a safe exit. He concluded that the snake had probably swallowed an animal, was lazily digesting it, and wasn't hungry at the time.

## American Medical Missionaries Also Felt the Stress

Everyone on the mission field feels the results of culture shock and fatigue—even Dr. Zimmerman. We were so thankful for our Seventh Day Adventist doctors and their hospital. The hospital was nothing like your American image of a hospital. It was primitive compared to our modern hospitals, but the doctors were good.

However, after they experienced similar stresses, and when their patience gave out, they discarded their professional images and became "just people" like the rest of us.

The little daughter of a missionary fell and cut a gash in her forehead. Her mother, Jodie, took her to Dr. Zimmerman. Jodie was a little dominant in her personality, and on this occasion, she feared a scar on her daughter's forehead.

Dr. Zimmerman examined the wound and was preparing to treat it when Jodie said, "You can treat it with 'butterflies' (thin strips of tape) instead of stitches, can't you?"

Dr. Zimmerman stopped, looked at her, and asked in a somewhat cynical tone, "Do you think that is the best way to treat it?"

Jodie was a little offended by his attitude and replied, "Well, I don't know. You're the doctor."

"Yes, but you are giving the orders."

One day I went for a check-up. Dr. Zimmerman was treating Ethiopian patients in a little makeshift, outpatient clinic. There was a long line of people standing outside, waiting to see him. He had been treating patients and performing surgery for thirty-six hours without relief. He was not a happy doctor.

He said, "You think your kids get on your nerves? Well, just look out there at what I have to put up with. One man was just in here trying to make me give his wife an injection of medicine that he brought with him. I couldn't make him understand that I couldn't do that because it might be dangerous. I didn't know what was in that bottle. If I gave her an injection that killed her, they would lock me up." He was suffering. That happened a short time after Christmas.

Someone had sent me some comic strips that included "Peanuts." Lucy was acting as the doctor, and Charlie Brown was her patient. She was irritable, and he asked her why she was being so mean to him. The picture showed her mouth open as wide as the ocean and her eyebrows were frowning to show her frustration.

She screamed, "Well, we doctors have our post-season letdowns too, you know."

It reminded me of my visit to Dr. Zimmerman. So I clipped it and gave it to him the next time I saw him. It relieved his tension momentarily and produced a smile.

LaMoin at four months old

LaMoin and her Mother

LaMoin at five years old
in Los Angeles

LaMoin at four years old in Los Angeles

LaMoin's Dad, Mother and brother Jerry

LaMoin's High School graduation picture

Bill and LaMoin's wedding picture

Cunningham's home in Ethiopia

(from L – R) Dinkanish, Shaleen, Yeshi holding Greg

Bill, LaMoin, Wyvonna,
Greg, and Shaleen

Wyvonna, Greg, and
Shaleen—our second
Christmas in Ethiopia

Bill and LaMoin in Ethiopian clothes

LaMoin petting a Cheetah at the Palace

LaMoin on visitation

Bill and LaMoin having lunch in Yeshi's home

LaMoin grinding grain

Pouring the batter for injerra

Yeshi stokes the fire

Yeshi placed the lid on and waits for it to cook

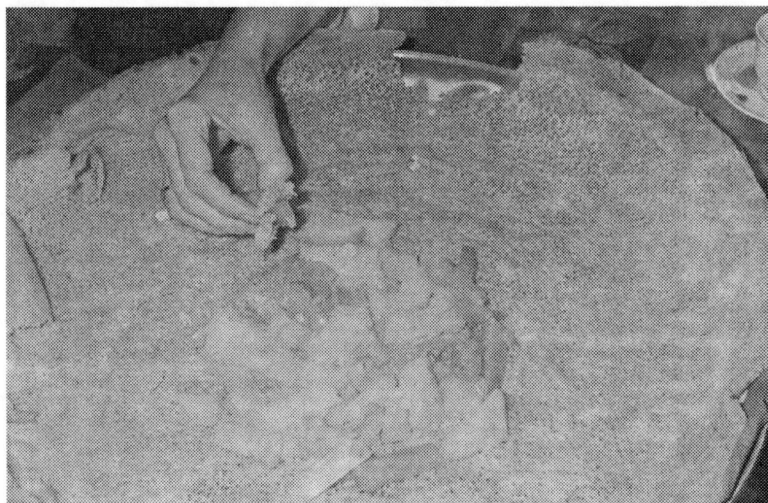

The proper way to eat injerra and wat

LaMoin at the Idal open market

LaMoin shaking hands with Haile Selassie

Bill and some members in front of church

LaMoin, Wyvonna, Shaleen, and Greg

The Cunninghams tour the Acropolis in Greece

LaMoin carries Wyvonna in the open market

# CHAPTER 12

# Dangerous Experiences

Traveling the unpaved roads of Ethiopia was very dangerous. We were returning home from a mission trip and were up in the very high mountains. Up ahead, we noticed a big herd of extra-large baboons running across the field.

Normally, I would have been squealing with delight, but this time I could not get excited. I was scared for my life. No, no. I was not afraid of the baboons, even though they were dangerous. In that same area, a large pack of them had thrown big stones at one of our missionaries. But at this particular time, I was afraid of our van running off the side of the mountain.

Our brakes had gone out, and we were in mountains that looked like the Rockies. The roads were all gravel, very narrow, winding, and had no guardrails to stop a car from plunging thousands of feet into the valley below.

We were an hour from home when the brake line had broken. We weren't traveling fast, so Bill used the gears to slow the van down. We were thankful that we had met very few cars. Most of the drivers drove down the middle of the road, and we had to always negotiate the possibility of meeting one on a curve.

We were doing fine, until we saw the cattle crossing the road. We barely missed one cow and miraculously made it through the herd. We were breathing sighs of relief as we approached Addis, when suddenly, a group of native dancers, with wild costumes and big lion headdresses, jumped into the road. They were performing some kind of tribal dance as their bodies bounced up and down and around in circles.

Normally, it would have been one of those coveted moments when we would have stopped and started shooting—with the camera! But we couldn't stop! Bill was blowing the horn and using the gears. I am sure I stopped breathing for a few minutes. I was in a state of mental panic. I just knew that we were going to hit them. Bill did everything to stop or to get them out of the road, but nothing worked. Finally, we braced ourselves for the collision.

"I guess we'll just have to kill a few of them," Bill said. They jumped from the road just before getting struck by the van. We are still not sure why they would not get out of the road. Maybe they were demon-possessed and were trying to get us killed. We can only use our imaginations. After we could breathe again, we thanked God for His protection.

We were on another trip when we had a similar experience, but this time the pedestrian became the victim. We were returning from a country mission station where we had been for a few days with the missionaries. An American army sergeant, Jim, and his family were with us.

We were driving a little Volkswagen car, and Jim was in an Army Land Rover. He needed gas and, since his vehicle was faster than ours was, he decided that he would speed up and get to a gas station beyond the little village we were approaching. He was to wait there until we caught up with him.

We had Yeshi and the children in the car, were relaxed, and enjoying the ride. We were traveling about forty miles an hour as we approached the village. Bill slowed down as we saw a man walking on the right side of the road. A big truck was parked on the side of the road, and the man was walking next to it.

Bill blew the horn to let him know that we were approaching, assuming that he would stay on the right side of the road near the truck. Suddenly, the man dashed across the road in front of us! Bill went to the right, and the man ran back in front of us. Bill steered left, and he ran to the left, back in front of us. All of this maneuvering happened within seconds.

I screamed, "Bill, you're going to hit him."

Blap! He was staring at me through the shattered windshield. I froze, closed my eyes, and screamed. Bill jumped from the car.

"Is he dead?" I cried, still holding my eyes closed. I opened them for a quick second, and he was gone from the hood. I was afraid to look on the ground by my side of the car; for fear that I would see him bleeding to death.

I had visions of Bill being dragged off to some filthy Ethiopian prison, where he would never get out. Of course, I was concerned about the man, too, but my selfishness prevailed.

"No, he's not dead," Bill said. "He's standing over by the car."

I was so paralyzed by fear that I had failed to notice the tire that he carried on his head. When the little "beetle" hit him, it caught him just above his shins, and he hit the hood, but the tire hit the rim of the windshield and shattered it. I thought his head hit the windshield. Our guardian angel kept the glass from falling in on us, so we were not hurt.

Quickly, hundreds of people gathered around the car. Some were telling him to lie down and pretend to be "asleep." If he was hurt, they could all profit greatly by the money that they could extract from the white man. There was shouting and confusion. I still sat in the car, half-numb with fear.

Within a few minutes, the local policemen were there, along with the mayor. They were like vultures over the prey—us! Yeshi jumped from the car and proceeded to defend us. Bless her heart! She was called many names by her own people for telling the truth and defending the white man. They called her a white woman (which was an insult to an Ethiopian). But she was spunky, and they didn't bother her. She was like a bulldog in our defense.

As the shouting and arguing continued I sat in the car crying. My nerves had taken a beating. An Ethiopian man walked up to the car and asked, "What's wrong?" I ignored him, but I was thinking, "You idiot. We almost killed this man, and my husband is going to be put into prison where the water is knee-high and filthy. They will starve him and never let him out, and you ask me what's wrong?"

Suddenly, I realized that I had an uncontrollable problem—dysentery! Oh, no! There was no place to go to a

146

toilet! What was I going to do? "Please God," I prayed, "Help me! Don't let me lose control here, please!" I was in a panic. When you gotta go, you gotta go, but there was no place to go—except in the car. Perish the thought! What was I going to do?

Bill sent a boy to the gas station to get Jim. He quickly came in his Land Rover and viewed the situation. Being a career soldier, he immediately arrived at a solution.

"Bill," he said calmly, "I'll just jump up on top of this Rover and empty a few rounds of ammo with my M-2 Carbine, and when I do, you jump in your car and get out of here."

"Oh, no," Bill pleaded. "I'm in enough trouble now. Please don't do that."

Finally, the policeman decided to take the man to the hospital to have him examined. Everyone looked—the man was gone! He had slipped away during the argument. (I don't know if he went away to die in peace, if he was hurting and didn't feel up to the fight, or was scared.) It was then decided that we would go to the little local clinic with the mayor and policemen, to see if he was there.

At this point, I was more concerned about my problem than I was about the injured man. I was rejoicing about going to the clinic. At least maybe I could find a toilet!

We arrived at the clinic, but the man was not there. The authorities looked very puzzled. How could they arrest this white man when there was no victim? (I'm sure they were seeing their possible fortune disappear.) They concluded that they didn't have a case and let Bill leave. I went to the toilet, then we got in the car and left.

Bill drove a safe distance, stopped, and finished knocking the windshield out so he could see, and we drove on toward Addis. The rest of the trip was stressful. Driving on dirt and gravel roads without a windshield was hazardous, but our guardian angel protected us until we arrived safely home.

Bill was angry later because we had just had our little Volkswagen freshly painted. Now it had a broken windshield and four dents in the hood where the man's elbows and knees hit.

A missionary friend of ours was driving along a country road toward Addis when a man ran in front of his car, and he hit him. The impact knocked him into a ditch, and the missionary quickly started backing up, to see if the man was hurt. The man in the ditch saw the car coming back, quickly jumped up, and ran away. I guess he thought the driver was coming back to run over him.

## I Tried to Kill Him

We recuperated and resumed our normal routine without any exciting events, until the day a stranger invaded our home. Bill was gone, and the kids and I were alone. I was so frightened. I knew that I didn't want him to come close to the kids or me, so I ran to my purse, grabbed the little pistol that I carried and shot at him—with tear gas! I really wasn't stupid, just panic-stricken! I didn't know what to do. I thought that if I could blind him with tear gas maybe I could outsmart him.

The tear gas hurt me more than the stranger. Thank the Lord, Bill walked in during the panic and took over for me.

He closed the bedroom door so the rat couldn't get out. Oh! Did I fail to mention that the stranger was the biggest rat I've ever seen? He was the size of a cat—well, in my condition he looked that big. I don't know which of us was scared the most, the rat or me!

He chased that rat all over the room. The rat ran around the bed, behind the bed, on the bed, and Bill was right behind him with a poker. He was sweating and exhausted by the time he finally cornered the rat and ran the poker into him, squashing him against the wall. I'm sure by this time that death was a pleasant escape for the rat.

A short time after the rat incident, Bill decided that I needed to know how to defend myself if it ever became a necessity—because of people, not rats! He had handguns and a .22 Hornet rifle with a hair trigger. We started going into the country to target practice. After a short time, I would stand on a bridge, high above the water, with the rifle. Bill would toss in a little ball of foil, and I would shoot it out of the water.

We were out target practicing with the pistols one day and it began to rain. We ran for cover in a large culvert that went under the road and back into the mountain. When we got inside, we noticed an Ethiopian man squatted down inside the culvert. Bill opened his coat to shake off the water, and when he did, the Ethiopian saw those two pistols strapped to his sides. We only saw a black streak as he ran out the other end of the culvert. We didn't mean to scare the poor fellow, but we came to the conclusion later that he had probably gone into the culvert when he heard the shooting because he was afraid of getting shot.

I really never feared bodily harm from the Ethiopians. They always treated me with the greatest of respect, especially after they knew that I was a pretty good shot with a gun.

# CHAPTER 13

# Learning to be a Mom in Africa

I had read many books on raising children but nothing was included about being a mom in Africa. There were so many strange things to deal with in this country. I was so afraid that the girls would contract some terrible disease. In the meanwhile, being pregnant and fearing about my care during delivery was also a strain. Our two precious daughters were also experiencing some culture shock.

## Shaleen Almost Died

Shaleen became very sick when she was about eight months old. She had dysentery, vomiting, and couldn't keep anything on her stomach. One night she was worse, and I took her to a nurse in the building. She said, "You must get this baby to the doctor. She is suffering from dehydration."

We didn't have a car yet, so Bill ran to get John, who bounded up the stairs to our apartment. "Come on. I'll take you to the hospital." John was a tank driver in the Korean War, and I wondered later if that was why he always drove as if he was in a battle.

We were racing to the hospital. John was also frightened. He was driving so fast, screeching around the corners, and I was scared. I kept begging him to slow down. I think I finally got on his nerves, and he shouted, "We've got to get this baby to the hospital or she might die."

"Yes, but I don't want to kill her before we get there," I cried.

We arrived safely, and the Ethiopian doctor took her into the examining room. He took a dirty spoon, washed it under the water faucet, and started to give her some medicine. Bill and I refused to let him give her medicine from the polluted spoon and walked out.

We then went to the Seventh Day Adventist Hospital, where a missionary doctor treated her. The doctor thought about admitting her into the hospital but finally decided to let us take her home. He gave us medicine and instructed us about giving it to her.

She had contracted amebic dysentery, probably from the lady who was cleaning the house. Ameba was very bad, and many of the Ethiopians died with it. If it wasn't killed, it would eat the bowels. The stools would become bloody and make the patient so weak and dehydrated that death would follow.

The doses had to be very strong to kill the bug, and because Shaleen was so young, the doctor couldn't give her enough of the medicine to kill the ameba. He had her on treatment for a long time. She lost so much weight, and we thought several times that she would not survive.

During her illness, I quit language school to stay home and take care of her. I didn't trust the house help. I knew that the language was important, but not more important than my children were. She finally started to improve, but she remained thin for a very long time.

## Kids Cause Gray Hair

Wyvonna had never been around dark-skinned people, and she was a bit afraid of them. One day, we were waiting in the car while Bill was in a shop. She was standing on the seat, looking out the window. Two well-dressed young men passed the car, saw her, and one of them came up and started talking to her.

She said, "*Heed* ("go" in Amharic), monkey." I could have died! I don't know why she said that. She had a stuffed monkey and she must have associated the color. I was so happy that he had a sense of humor, because he understood English.

While we were having dinner one evening, Wyvonna left the table, opened the door, stepped outside, and closed the door. I jumped from my chair to get her, and then I heard a loud thump downstairs. I almost went into labor!

Bill came running also. I just knew she had fallen down the opening in the staircase that went to the bottom floor (remember, we were on the fourth floor). I didn't hear her cry, and I was afraid to look. Finally, I was able to move, and I looked behind me. To my relief, there she stood, backed up against the wall, holding her doll (probably wondering what all the excitement was about). I stood crying and said, "How do people raise children without going crazy?"

I was doing some work in the kitchen one day when I heard John softly calling my name from the parking lot below our apartment. I went to the open window and looked down. He looked as if he had seen a ghost but was trying to be calm. "Now, don't panic. Wyvonna is leaning out of the dining room window. Move quietly, because you might frighten her, and she will fall."

My heart skipped a few beats as I went to the dining room and saw her balancing herself on the window ledge, looking down at John. I was able to get her out of the window before she fell four floors down onto a concrete parking lot.

After that incident, Bill and I knew that we had to move to a safer place for the children. We would wait until after our baby was born and then start looking for another place to live.

## Our First Ethiopian Christmas Tree

Christmas was near and we wanted to have a good Christmas for Wyvonna. She was two now and would enjoy it. It was hard to find a Christmas tree. However, there was a nice evergreen tree growing behind our parking lot, on the other side of the fence. The top of the tree grew up above our fence. It was beautiful and didn't seem to belong to anyone. Besides, the Ethiopians were not really conscious about their landscape when they were striving to put food on the table.

Bill cut the top, and we set it up in our apartment. We had fun decorating it with things that we had brought from the States. It was beautiful.

154

John came up to see us, and his eyes nearly popped out as he looked at our tree.

"Where did you get that tree?"

"At the back of the building," Bill said.

"Man, I've had my eye on that tree for weeks, and I was afraid to cut it! You could be in serious trouble for cutting that tree." He wasn't really a coward, so we really got the tree due to his procrastination.

That tree helped to provide the atmosphere we all needed to keep from being too homesick, and no trouble ever came. I suppose only the Lord, John, Bill, and I knew that he cut it and none of us was telling.

## I Hate Worms

I was so paranoid about my children getting germs. I made the cleaning woman mop the floors with a strong disinfectant every day. I was extra careful about the babies' bottles and all the food. Everything had to be clean and sterilized.

Most of the Africans had stomach worms, and the ones who had enough knowledge took treatments every six months to kill the worms. The treatment made them very sick for a day afterwards.

As a child, I would get sick and couldn't eat if someone mentioned worms. My brothers thought it was funny and would do it as often as they could without my mother knowing. For that reason, I could never eat spaghetti.

Now, here I was, living in a country where it was common for the missionaries to discuss various problems at the dinner table and many times it involved worms. I had not overcome my phobia so I lost weight even though I was pregnant. I would lose my appetite if I heard about worms. The things that appalled people in other countries were looked upon as commonplace by the missionaries. There was always a strange story to tell. One friend told about a worker on his interior compound that had a worm that periodically crawled across his eyeball, which was the only time that it could be removed. I hated the thought of my children having worms!

When Wyvonna had her second birthday, Mother sent her a little necklace that she enjoyed wearing. But it went missing, and I thought she had taken it off and lost it. However, one day, she went to the bathroom and called me to come help her wipe her bottom. To my horror, there was a glob of something hanging out of her. My first thought was—you guessed it—*worms*!

I froze. I couldn't touch her. I stood and stared at the poor child. She looked at me with child-like confusion as I stood motionless in the bathroom door. Poor baby wondered why I wasn't helping her.

Yeshi was gone for the day, so I finally forced myself to take a piece of toilet paper to pull the glob out of my little helpless child. It took all the courage I had. I took a deep breath, held the paper, prayed, and made contact. I expected them to move, and I prayed, "Lord, please, make them stay still." Then I felt something hard.

I determined that the glob was not worms, so I quickly rinsed it off under some water. It was a chain! She had swallowed her necklace and it had passed through her! God certainly watches over our children. I was so thankful that the chain had passed without causing a problem, and I was equally happy that it was not worms!

I could laugh about it later, but it did not cure my phobia. Every time the children got pale or white around the mouth, I would shrink in fear. I had always heard that paleness around the mouth indicated worms. I don't know if that is true or not.

## The *Idals* Spat on My Baby

We went to visit Delmar and Helen Powell on their interior station. They took us to a large, open market in the desert. There were hundreds of *Idal* tribes people there who were buying and trading their goods. The *Idals* live in the desert and wear very few clothes. They had chopped leaves and rancid butter in their hair and on their body. They put the butter on their bodies to help protect them from the sun. The leaves were for beauty. The smell was terrible. There is no smell to compare to an *Idal* open market! I don't know who smelled the most, the people or the animals. Stinking, old camels lay everywhere, chewing their cud. Have you ever been close to a camel? They are so ugly! Pitiful!

There were people sitting all over the ground with their items that they were trying to sell or trade. Some had food items, clothes, kitchenware, and various other things. Others had animals for sale or trade.

The sun was hot, and the sights and smell were not enjoyable, but the experience was worth the misery. As we started into the midst of the people and the animals, I picked Wyvonna up to carry her and to protect her from some of the things that I saw on the ground.

As we walked among the people they would spit on her! One man spit at her and hit me. I was thinking about sending a few of them in on God unexpectedly. The very idea! Spitting on my baby! I could only imagine all the germs that were contained in that spittle. I was trying to shield her, and my arm was wet.

"Why are they spitting on us?" I asked Delmar. I was upset.

"It's their custom to show their approval and blessing for the child," he explained. Who needs it? Some customs in a new culture are just not acceptable!

## Paradise

John (our missionary friend) was excited as he pleaded with us to go with him to his newfound "paradise." He said, "Bill, this place is beautiful. It's a regular paradise. You've got to come. We'll take the families, and we'll have a picnic and go fishing. It's a great place to fish."

We liked to experience new things, so we agreed to go. John and Gail and their two children, and Bill and the girls and I loaded into the cars. We took food, fishing equipment, and of course, cameras. This was before Greg was born, and I was about seven months pregnant!

We drove up into the mountains for about two hours, maybe longer. John pulled off the road and started getting out.

Bill parked, got out of the car, and asked, "Where is this paradise?" All we could see was a rugged mountain.

"Just over that ridge," John excitedly replied.

Bill and I looked at each other skeptically. We got the children and the gear and followed John and Gail. We climbed over rocks and ditches until we reached the top of the "ridge," which was more like a mountain. From time to time, Bill would say, "Are you OK?" I was doubtful at times, but I had to see this "paradise" of John's.

We finally reached the top. John was ecstatic as he pointed down the cliff to a lake with a scraggly, rocky area next to the water. Now, we had to climb down to that area.

When we had managed to get to the bottom of the hill, I looked at Bill and remarked, "This is paradise?"

"Doesn't look like paradise to me," he said. "Only John could think this is paradise."

It was time for lunch, so we prepared our food and ate. John and Bill started fishing. When we weren't running after the kids, Gail and I relaxed on the rocks.

While they were fishing, an Ethiopian boy, about eleven or twelve years old, came up to them and started talking. He was carrying an expensive fishing rod and reel that we knew that most poor Ethiopians couldn't afford, especially children. John looked at the equipment and asked, "Where did you get that rod and reel?"

The boy gave some explanation that wasn't acceptable. Suddenly John yelled, "You're a liar. You stole that from my friend." (He and a doctor friend had gone fishing there, and the doctor had his rod and reel stolen.) He grabbed it and slapped the kid in the head. The kid ran off over the mountain.

Bill looked at me and said, "Let's get out of here." John didn't want us to leave.

Bill said, "John, you're going to be in serious trouble, and I don't want to keep LaMoin and the kids here. You and Gail better come with us."

John refused, saying, "Aw, he won't do anything. The kid is a thief. I know this is Doc's rod and reel. He was the one who stole it."

We left, and by the time we reached the car, the whole village was coming toward us, with the kid leading the pack. Bill hurried and started the car, and we took off.

John and Gail came home that night and told the rest of the story. Just as we had expected, the whole village descended on him. Only John could have talked his way out of that situation without getting killed. But he finally proved (I don't know how) that the kid had stolen the rod and reel, and the people let him go.

## I Even Learned Customs in the Beauty Shop

Believe it or not, all of Ethiopia was not primitive. We had beauty shops in Addis, and many of the hairdressers were Greeks and Italians.

One day while I was having my hair done the Ethiopian woman who owned the shop had some *injerra* and *wat* brought in for her lunch. She came and asked me to eat some of it. I had still not developed a taste for it, so I thanked her but refused it. She would not take no for an answer and persisted until I ate a little of the food.

Later, my Italian hairdresser told me that it was a custom that an Ethiopian will never eat in the presence of a pregnant woman without first giving her some of the food. They believe that the baby will be marked if the mother smells the food and feels hunger but doesn't eat some of it. The lady would never have eaten her lunch if I had refused it.

## Our New Family Member Arrived

Soon I would be ready to deliver our third child. To my great relief, I would have an American missionary doctor and be in a mission hospital.

It was getting increasingly more difficult to climb four flights of stairs, especially since the baby had dropped so low two months prior (probably due to the bumpy roads and the lack of an elevator). I would be so happy to deliver.

I went to Dr. Zimmerman for a check-up, and he said the baby was ready to be born. One problem—he was leaving the city for a few days. With my permission, he induced labor so he could be there for the delivery. I was not about to let someone else deliver my baby. I trusted him.

I had experienced difficult deliveries with Wyvonna and Shaleen so I told him that I wanted to be put to sleep. To my utter surprise, due to his Adventist church beliefs, he could not put me to sleep for the birth. (They still obey the Old Testament. When God cursed Eve, He said that women would have pain in childbearing.)

I knew that I was in trouble! I said, "You don't understand. I must be put to sleep. My deliveries are hard, and I can't stand pain."

"Oh, I'll give you some locals, and you'll be OK. You won't feel any pain."

Wanna bet? I thought I liked him.

The hospital was old and simple, but it was clean. I had a small private room. The bed had an old iron headboard and footboard. It was in this room that I labored before I was ready for delivery. Bill said that I almost turned a lot of Ethio-

pians white with my screaming, which is not their custom.
Hang their custom! I was doing what came naturally.

When I was ready to deliver, they took me to the delivery room, past a ward with Ethiopian women who were in labor. They were *sitting* in little individual "stalls," not making a sound! (They were fortunate to be in the hospital. Most of the women worked until time for delivery.)

The African way of delivery was hard. A man would get on each side, take the woman's arms, and jump her up and down until the baby "plopped" (which was their terminology). Many babies were severely injured during this barbaric delivery. But these women did not show pain.

I still don't understand how they could endure it, but it wasn't going to stop me from releasing my tension! I was having this baby American style—screaming and all! (Don't try to convince me that the modern child birth classes could have helped.) The doctor gave me locals, but I couldn't tell that they helped to kill any pain.

A nurse stood behind my head with a gas mask. During a contraction, he would permit her to give me a little gas. When she put the mask over my nose and mouth, I grabbed her wrist with a death grip, held the mask there, and breathed as fast as I could, hoping to get enough to put me to sleep. But she would pry it away from me.

Gregory William was born on Tuesday, February 23, 1965 at 1:05 A.M. The doctor said, "It's a boy!" He had been telling me that he thought it was a girl. Of course, we had no ultra sounds back in those days.

I groaned, "Thank You, Lord."

Bill adored our two daughters, but he wanted a boy so badly. We knew that this child would be our last because of some female problems that I had experienced for a long time.

After Greg was born, my teeth were popping together, and I couldn't stop them. I was shaking, and felt that I was freezing to death.

"What's wrong with me?" I asked the doctor.

"You'll be OK," he replied as he moved more quickly than I had ever seen him move.

He gave me an injection, started an IV, and covered me with blankets and hot water bottles. He seemed almost in a panic. After I was stabilized, he told Bill that I was going into shock, and he was afraid for awhile that he might lose me. I think that he was sorry that he had not listened to me. After I was out of danger, they took me to my room. Greg was put in a little bassinet and placed in the room with me.

The next morning, I called my Ethiopian nurse to come change his diaper. He had a bowel movement, and I could not move from my bed to wash and change him. She was very sweet and helpful. She dipped the washcloth into my glass of drinking water, washed him, and changed his diaper. However, she did not remove the water when she left.

Later, I asked for some water. The nurse looked a little confused as she pointed to my glass and said, "You have some water." I reminded her that she had washed Greg with that water. It caused a bit of concern for me. I thought, "If the nurse is that careless, what about the kitchen help?"

My concerns were confirmed when I contracted dysentery later. Naturally, I wasn't surprised. I told Dr. Zimmerman. He just smiled and said to the nurse, "Give her some bismuth and opium." This was the common and best treatment, which was on every missionary's medicine shelf.

## I Couldn't Walk Up the Stairs

After one week Greg and I left the hospital, but I was still in pretty bad shape. I was experiencing pain and extreme soreness. I knew that I could never climb those stairs to our apartment. Bill and Denton devised a plan. They put me on a chair and carried me up the stairs. I felt sorry for them as they huffed, puffed, and rested between flights. It is more difficult to breathe in the high altitude, and carrying me up four flights of steps was extremely difficult (I wasn't skinny). I appreciated them, because I could not have gotten home any other way. (I love elevators! I never take them for granted. It should be a crime to build a building without an elevator!)

Greg was a healthy, beautiful baby with large, blue eyes. He cried very little. Wyvonna and Shaleen loved him immediately. Wyvonna was fascinated and tried to climb into the carriage with him. One day she succeeded. The carriage tipped over, and Greg fell on his head. He survived without any damage.

I was so happy to be home so I could take a good bath. The shower at the hospital was out of order. I had to put soap on my body and then pour pans of water over me to rinse off. At least I felt clean and refreshed. And I was thankful that I was able to be in a mission hospital with a good American doctor, even if he wouldn't put me to sleep!

Greg was born on February twenty-third, and Shaleen turned one on February twenty-fifth. Wyvonna was then almost two and a half years old. Yes, I had my hands full while trying to adjust to living in Africa and learning the language.

I dropped out of formal language study, but I was studying at home with a tutor. However, I was learning the most from Yeshi. She didn't speak much English, and since I had to communicate with her, I was forced to learn Amharic. I was never fluent, but I could manage to make them understand me.

I regained my strength quickly. I was enjoying our little family and trying my best to be the best mom that I could be.

## Customs Was a Rip-off

After Greg was born, a box arrived from a church in the States. The customs declaration, with the required list of contents, was taped to the outside of the box. They sent things for the baby, including diaper pins, lotion, powder, and other items.

Bill went to the customs section of the post office where they were holding the box. Since the list of contents was on the outside, he refused to open the box, in spite of the insistence of the postal worker. When they made us open a box, they would then quote a high amount of customs tax to us. Most of the time we couldn't afford to pay the amount or the contents were not even worth it.

After the box was refused, they would make us pay the postage to return it to the sender. This postage was also high, so the government made money either way. Bill tried to reason with the man, but he finally refused the box and told them to send it back—at their expense. However, they usually held the box for a few days before returning it, hoping that the recipient would have a change of mind.

Once we received a Sears catalog. The customs man saw a pair of men's shoes on the back cover with a price of forty dollars. He thought that's what the catalog cost so he said the customs would be forty dollars—100% of an advertisement. See what we had to deal with?

I was so disappointed when Bill told me that he had told them to return the box. I really needed those things. I was feeling much better, so I decided that I would try to get it out at a decent price. Maybe I would be lucky and get a good customs officer (the individual determined the amount of customs).

I went into the customs room and waited my turn. There were many foreigners in the room who were having the same problems in trying to get their boxes.

My turn came and I stepped up to the "batter's plate" for my experience. The man brought the box out and asked me to open it. I falsely pretended to be sweet and ignorant. I showed him the list of contents and told him that I had just had a new baby and that a church had sent these things to me. I tried to appeal to his sensitive nature, fully aware that he didn't have one.

He insisted that I open it, and I kept telling him that the list explained what was inside. Unfortunately, he was the kind who wanted everyone to know how important he was. He was talking loudly so everyone could hear his intelligent reasoning. By this time, he and I shared the spotlight. I knew that I had lost the war, but I did not intend to lose this battle.

He arrogantly said, "Well, for example, this says, 'diaper pins,' but there are many different kinds of these pins. There are cloth ones, paper ones, wooden ones, metal ones, etc."

I reached into my purse, took out a diaper pin, held it up in his face, and firmly said, "This is a diaper pin. Have you ever seen one made of cloth, paper, or wood?"

There was a roar of laughter from all the other frustrated foreigners. While the embarrassment and anger was building up for the explosion I said goodbye to my box and walked out of the building. I felt pretty good.

Now, your self-righteous attitude is probably criticizing me saying, "A missionary shouldn't act like that." Go experience it for a few months, and then let's compare notes.

# CHAPTER 14

## Unpleasant Memories

⁂

*I* had been under medical treatment for some female problems before leaving America. Dr. Zimmerman had continued treating me for a chronic infection in the uterus, but it would not heal. One month after Greg was born he told me that I needed to have a hysterectomy because the infection was chronic and that it was a miracle that it had not developed into cancer. He counseled (medically) with Bill and me, and we agreed to have the surgery. He also said that giving birth to another baby would be very dangerous to my health.

As soon as I had regained some of my strength, I entered the hospital for surgery. Dr. Zimmerman consulted with a German gynecologist who came and examined me. They both agreed that the hysterectomy was needed, but the night before my scheduled surgery, Dr. Zimmerman came to my room.

"I cannot do the hysterectomy tomorrow. One of my colleagues here in the hospital (and in the same mission) doesn't agree with the surgery. The German doctor and I showed him the reports and told him why it was necessary, but he has threatened to report me to the Medical Board in the US if I perform the surgery. I could lose my medical license."

"Why is he doing this?" I asked.

"He says that you are too young to have the surgery and that we are doing it for birth control. We know you need it, but I will just be honest with you. You and I are both missionaries, and we know that jealousy exists. He and I were in medical school together, and then we came here as missionaries. I have advanced more quickly (he was in charge of the hospital), and he thinks he should have my position, so he does everything he can to cause me trouble. I am sorry that you have to be involved, but I know he will carry out his threat, and I cannot take that risk."

"So, do I just go home?" I was mad by this time, not at Dr. Zimmerman but the other doctor.

"No. The gynecologist and I have agreed that it is dangerous for you to have another child. You have already been prepared for surgery so I am going to do a tubal ligation now. You will have to have the hysterectomy in the near future, but I want to make sure you do not get pregnant again. I will continue to treat the infection in one last effort to heal it."

The next morning, six weeks after Greg was born, I went in for the surgery. Dr. Zimmerman had decided to give me an epidural instead of putting me to sleep. (Don't ask me; I don't know why.) I trusted him, even if he would not put me to sleep when Greg was born.

I had no anxieties—until I saw the size of that needle. He almost had to restrain me! I have never seen a needle as big as that one! I had never done anything bad to him. Why was he torturing me?

He said, "Now just relax. This looks awful, but it won't hurt very much." Fine for him to say; it wasn't his spine!

Bill asked if he could watch the operation and Dr. Zimmerman said yes. I know it was unorthodox, and no doctor in America would permit it. But we were in Africa. Everything was done differently there.

As I lay on the operating table Bill walked in with Dr. Zimmerman, all scrubbed and sterile, in a surgical cap and gown. I had some shots so I was feeling pretty drugged. I knew what was going on, but I didn't care. It was a good thing, because as he made the incision, I heard him explaining everything to Bill.

"See, just a nice, clean cut. Now I have to spread the flesh and hold it open with these clamps."

He continued working and talking to Bill. "Now, this is a kidney. Here's her bladder, (etc.)."

They were just having a great time exploring my anatomy. I felt no pain but became a bit nauseated when I could feel something being pressed up toward my diaphragm. "I feel sick in my stomach."

He continued working and calmly said to the nurse, "Remove that sponge." Thank you!

Even in my stupor, I realized that Bill was fully enjoying himself, and he was doing great! Dr. Zimmerman finished and was closing me when I heard a loud thump on the floor to my right. I groggily looked for Bill, but he was not there.

"Was that my husband?" I drawled.

Dr. Zimmerman acted as if nothing had happened and calmly exclaimed as he continued closing, "Yes, he fainted. He'll be OK. Nurse, open that door so he can get some fresh air."

After I was back in my room, Bill came in to see me. He was humiliated! While in the Korean War his eyes had seen much worse. Dr. Zimmerman consoled him by telling him that it was the smell of the blood that made him pass out. He said, "I've seen it happen many times in college. Students would pass out, one after another, and the instructor would just keep working. It's happened to me."

I stayed in the hospital for a few days and was released in time to go to church on Sunday, stitches and all. I taught my Sunday school class as if nothing unusual had happened. The work must go on. Was I crazy? The Bible does tell us that we are fools for Christ's sake. I guess that could be explained as one of those times.

## A Vacation in the Country

After I was feeling well and able to travel, we took a short vacation and went to visit our good friends, Delmar and Helen Powell. Their mission station was about six hours north from Addis. We were eager to see them because we always had many laughs together, and I needed a few at that time.

They lived in a house that they had built themselves, up in the middle of the mountains. They had never built anything before, but missionaries must learn to do many things. Delmar bought a book that taught him how to put the house together, and they labored long months to finish it while living in their tin hut. Many people think missionaries are a bit inferior, can't make it in the States, and that's why they go to the mission field. The opposite is true; missionaries can do almost anything when the need arises. The mission field is no place for the sissy or loser.

The men went out to kill some fresh meat—wild boar—while Helen and I visited.

## Please God, Don't Let Her Fall in the Hole

They had an outdoor toilet that Del had built. He had dug the hole exceptionally deep, trying for a higher degree of sanitation and had done an excellent job. It was a *nice* outhouse! I am from Arkansas and lived in the country so I know a good outhouse when I see one!

I usually never let the girls out of my sight, but while Helen and I visited, they had managed to slip away from me. I heard Wyvonna crying and calling me. As usual, I ran in a panic to see what was wrong.

Shaleen was locked inside the toilet! She was crying. She was so young that it was difficult to make her follow instructions, especially since she was scared half to death.

"Don't get up on the bench, honey. Stay by the door. Don't cry; Mommy will get the door open. You will be fine."

As I tried to keep her calm only the power of God kept me from going ballistic! My imagination and fear kicked

173

in. If she falls into that hole, she will drown in all that "stuff." If you've never been in an outdoor toilet, ask someone who has to describe it to you! Ugh. I shuddered at the very thought.

We kept praying, talking, and working until we were able to get the door open. Finally, we got her out, and she was in better shape than I was.

## The Pigs Almost Got Delmar

While we were living through our nightmare, the men had an experience that could have been fatal but later provided many laughs for us in the future years. They had separated in the forest, and Del found a hole where the wild pigs lived. He called to Bill to shoot to scare them out.

It worked! They came out—straight for Del, which he had not anticipated. Because of fear and nerves, he couldn't get his gun to shoot until they were almost in his face. Now, I have never hunted wild boar, but from what the men tell me, they are fierce and dangerous animals. And to see several of these untamed, ferocious beasts running toward you is a bit unnerving. Delmar had seen the results of unfortunate animals that had been their victims. He knew that these animals could rip his body apart with their long tusks that curved up over their faces.

He could almost feel his fate. He was finally able to fire his gun just a couple of feet before they reached him, and they turned in another direction. It had been a close call. With God's protection, he had been spared from a horrible death. When they came home, Del was still as white as a sheet. Just another exciting day on the mission field!

By now you are saying, "Were they crazy? Why would they want to live in a place like that?" God has commanded us to go into all the world and preach the Gospel to every creature. (Matthew 28:19, 20), "Go ye therefore, and teach all nations, baptizing them in the name of the Father, and of the Son, and of the Holy Ghost: Teaching them to observe all things whatsoever I have commanded you: and, lo, I am with you always, even unto the end of the world." There were people in that area that had never heard about salvation, and the Powells felt burdened to tell them about Jesus Christ. Jesus left His heavenly home to come to Earth (a foreign land), and He suffered and died to provide salvation for us. How can we do less?

I have heard people say, "Those people (natives) are happy in their own ways. Why try to civilize and change them?" That seems to be a common belief in much of our Western world. Maybe I can change your mind.

## A Pagan Sacrifice

Delmar, Bill, and I rode horses (and a mule) up into the mountains to visit one of the villages where Del worked. Bare-breasted, dark-skinned women were cooking over open fires outside their one-room mud huts. The thatched roof helped to keep the rain from the little, dark, smoky rooms with mud floors. The only furniture they enjoyed were little three-legged stools, handcarved from tree stumps. Their beds were animal skins that were placed on the floor at night and rolled up during the day. If the weather was cold, they were used for a coat. The whole family lived, slept, and ate in that tiny one room.

Many little huts stood close together for protection. These tribes feared the season when young warriors became old enough to take a bride. To prove that they were men, they were required to kill a young man from another tribe and present his genitals to their chief. After a ceremony, the young warriors tied the trophies around their forehead and wore them so all could see that they had become a man.

Evil spirits and witchcraft were very real to these people who had no knowledge of the Lord Jesus Christ, who has all power over Satan. Can they really die when an enemy put an evil spell on them? Yes, and many did die. Satan has full control in this spiritual darkness. I can't explain the process or what really happened. Maybe they died because of fear. They absolutely gave up and accepted death as a reality when they were cursed.

Del showed us their place of worship, a large tree with evidence of recent meat sacrifices. The ritual included slaughtering an animal and sprinkling the blood all around the tree. Then they would leave the flesh for their god, an unseen giant snake that lived in the midst of the tree. They had to appease the snake and keep him happy so they would have good days and protection from their enemies. Superstition always exists when there is no knowledge of Christ.

A young man was gored by an ox one day. Del took him to the small local hospital. He was being treated when his family came. Fearing the modern doctor, they removed the young man from the hospital and took him back to their village to be treated by their medicine man (witch doctor). The young man died in a few days and went to a Christ-less Hell.

Do you think they are happy? I think not. They need the power of Christ to release them from their chains of bondage, fear, and suffering. That is why Jesus died. That's also why missionaries, in obedience to Him, leave the comfort of the Western world to serve in primitive and dangerous areas.

After our day of visitation, we headed down the mountain to the mission station. We were galloping the horses (and my mule) as we came down the mountain. Suddenly, I felt myself slipping to the side. I tried to straighten myself to an upright position but could not. I couldn't understand why when, suddenly, I landed on the ground!

The worker at the station had not properly cinched the saddle underneath the mule. It became loose and fell down, almost under the mule, and dumped me on my fanny! I wasn't hurt and we had a good laugh. That is another one of my experiences that I have never lived down.

How refreshing it was to later slip into Delmar's handmade shower and wash off the dust from the village. He was very creative and had rigged a chain that, when pulled, released a bucket of water from above. It was crude but effective.

# CHAPTER 15

# My Neighbors

The time came when we knew that we had to move from the apartment to another location. After many weeks of searching for a house, one of our Ethiopian friends told us about one. We immediately went to look at it.

We drove to the edge of Addis and all we saw were Ethiopian dwellings. Naturally, I was thinking, "Forget this." But we continued on. Leaving the main road, we saw another "road" built of large chunks of rock, placed loosely together. We bounced over these rocks to get to the house.

It was very impressive! Pink and green paint adorned the exterior. There was a large, open field on one side and an Ethiopian village of little mud huts on the other side. Around the house was a high stone wall with broken glass set in the concrete on top. This was to keep out hyenas— four-legged and "two-legged."

We opened the large iron gate and went inside. There was no grass on the yard. Instead, it was covered with small reddish stones of hardened volcanic ash, not a perfect place for children to play! Grass grows in Ethiopia so we thought we could later plant some seed and take care of that problem. (You have to be optimistic, even when it's ridiculous!) At least we didn't have to worry about the children falling down four floors to the concrete parking lot.

We walked inside. My eyes scanned the crudely built house. It certainly didn't compare to American houses, but it had plenty of room for our little family. The wood floors were better than concrete, and there was a kitchen with a single sink but nothing else. I was happy to see a bathroom with a modern toilet and tub. The walls were made of mud with a thin layer of concrete over them. The three bedrooms were plain but could be decorated to look cozy. The price was reasonable, so we rented it.

We moved into the house and were getting settled. I was trying to make it as comfortable as possible. I sewed curtains and bedspreads for all the beds. Bill even made a canopy over the girls' beds, and I made a beautiful, ruffled pink top for the canopy to match their spreads.

There was a building at the back that I could use for a laundry room. I had now acquired a coveted wringer washing machine from a Lutheran missionary who resigned and, went home. I don't know if culture shock won again or not. He said it was the mission. In fact, his very words were, "The Holy Spirit doesn't have a ghost of a chance in this mission." He didn't mean to blaspheme and was only using an old cliché with the wrong reference. Anyway, we bought the washing machine. It was a good one and I was so happy.

## A Cattle Market in Our Front Yard

The first Thursday after we moved I looked outside and was shocked to see hundreds of cows and people in front of our house and in the vacant field next door. They were there all day! It was a weekly cattle market—right in front of my gate!

Naturally, if you have five hundred cows practically in your front yard, you're going to have a mess left over. Right? I was mortified! "Oh, no. All that cow manure. Oh, the smell and the flies. Oh, Lord, why did I move here and get into this mess?"

My imagination kicked in, and I was entertaining some pretty disturbing thoughts. I knew that most cows had tuberculosis, and I even wondered if flies could transmit it. The American Army sent a special team of ten soldiers into Addis, and they stayed for a couple of weeks in a small local hotel. They ate the pastries in the restaurant, and when they left, six of them had contracted active tuberculosis. Doctors determined that it had come from the milk in the cream-filled pastries.

I hid in the house all day, and late that afternoon I ventured out to view the mess. To my utter amazement, the field was clean, and I saw no cow dung anywhere. No one would have known that hundreds of cows had been there all day.

The next week, I decided that I was going to see why everything had been so clean the week before. I was able to bring my discouragement and imagination into control and went outside to educate myself about an Ethiopian cattle market.

I saw the women going around picking up something. I took a closer look—you're right—they were picking up the cow dung. They were happily running to beat the others to a nice, fresh pile. I couldn't believe my eyes. They were using their hands to pick it up and flatten it out. They tried to get to a pile before the other women saw it. They were as excited as I would have been to find gold.

I later learned that the cow chips were a prized commodity. They took them home, let them dry for a few days, and then used them to build the fires for cooking their food. They also mixed the dung with mud and straw, shaped large "lids," and baked them. They used the lids to cover their food. Out of this material they also formed large flat pans that they placed on the fire to cook their bread on. When I heard that, I realized why the *injerra* tasted sour! (Just kidding.)

When the day ended and all the people and cows were gone, I went out to survey the aftermath. There wasn't a cow chip anywhere! You would never suspect that a cattle market had been in progress all day.

I was learning much about my new house and neighborhood. As I previously stated, we had a modern bathroom in that house. There was a small disadvantage. When we flushed the toilet, boiling hot water came into the tank. That wasn't altogether bad—we could enjoy a sauna in the bathroom!

We called the repairmen out to change the plumbing, and after several hours we had a normal bathroom again, without the sauna. It seems that the hot water pipe had inadvertently been run into the toilet tank. The Ethiopian plumber changed it upon our insistence, even though he could see no problem. It was water, wasn't it?

## A Demon-possessed Woman

We heard a terrible commotion outside and ran out to see what was happening. We saw a crowd of people watching a woman who was acting very strangely. She was naked and wore a fetish around her neck. She was throwing rocks at the people and screaming. She would fall down, crawl around on the rocks, and make weird noises.

When we walked out on the porch, she saw us and ran to our gate. She took hold of it and shook it with abnormal strength. She acted like an animal. We realized that this woman had many demons in her like the maniac that Jesus healed. We felt sorry for her, but we were not experienced in casting out demons. We knew that it could be very dangerous for a novice, so we watched as she turned and went down the road.

It grieved us that we couldn't help her and many others who were under the control of Satan. We were doing as much as we could to teach them and try to get them to believe in the power of Jesus to save their souls.

## Bill Preached to Malcolm X

When we lived in the mission building, Bill and the other resident missionaries took turns preaching in the chapel. One Sunday, it was Bill's turn to preach. Before the service began, John told Bill that Malcolm X was visiting in Nairobi. Malcolm X was a very well known Black Panther and black power activist from America.

John said, "Bill, I'm going to bring him to the service, and when I do, you really preach to him. He needs to get saved."

"Oh, you're just going to bring him to the service, huh? How are you going to do that?"

"I'll just go down to the hotel and get him." We laughed at him, because we felt that it wasn't possible for him to even get to see Malcolm X, especially to bring him to the service.

Bill was already preaching when John and Malcolm X walked into the chapel. He sat through most of the preaching. He didn't get saved, but he heard the plan of salvation. Two weeks later we read in the newspaper that he had been gunned down by his own race in New York.

## The Ministry Was Bearing Fruit

Bill rented a little Ethiopian house near our home and started a church. He daily visited in the village, distributed tracts, and held services on Sunday. Many people found new life in Christ, as he regularly knelt in the flea-infested dirt floor of that little native church and prayed with those who wanted to put their faith and trust in Jesus.

It was in our new home that I had the privilege of leading Yeshi to a saving knowledge of Christ. What a joy it was to see her set free from the bondage of Satan and her Coptic Church. Later, the Coptic priest visited her and insisted on her annual baptism to wash her sins away. Of course, there was a charge for this service. She joyfully informed him that Jesus had forgiven her sins and that she no longer needed the Coptic baptism.

God was blessing our efforts, and we were seeing much fruit. Bill had ten young men who were studying with him to become preachers. God also gave us the opportunity of working with some Americans.

The United States Army had a small group of people in Addis who were working in a mapping mission. Bill was asked by the commanding officer to come to their mess hall and hold services because they had no chaplain.

Bill agreed to hold Sunday services, and the CO made him the honorary chaplain. We went every Sunday to the mess hall. When we would arrive most of the guys would leave. Some stayed for the services, and we saw a few of them saved, but many of them didn't want any twinge of conscience to spoil their fun. Each Sunday I had to chase them out of the recreation room, clean up the beer bottles, and teach a Sunday school class for children there.

We really enjoyed working with these military people. We had enlisted men and officers in our meetings. They temporarily forgot their rank and worshipped together. I will never forget the blessings that we received from a little American black girl who was about ten years old. She loved to sing, and her favorite song was *It's Me, O Lord, Standing in the Need of Prayer*. She would sing with all of her heart as she swayed with the music.

Because Ethiopian law did not allow us to baptize anyone in that country, Bill had a large steel tank built to serve as a baptistery. He put it in our garage at home. We would have our baptisms in the garage, so that it would not be questioned.

The first time he filled the tank with water the sides bowed with the pressure of the water. He then built a wooden frame around it. He baptized many Americans and Ethiopians in that makeshift baptismal tank. You may wonder why we didn't use the river. Besides the danger of being reported to the government, the rivers were polluted with every kind of disease known to man.

Some of those who were saved are still actively serving God in the United States. We formed great friendships with the soldiers. They felt sorry for us because we couldn't get any of the goodies from the States. Of course, they had all of their food supplies shipped in from the US. They would always bring a can of American coffee or something when they came to visit.

One day, some of the guys came to our home and brought hot dogs, bologna, and potato chips. What a treat! Our children really enjoyed those hot dogs. We take so many things for granted in the States. In Ethiopia, even a candy bar was a prized treat.

## Tragedy of an American Soldier

We saw John Bunch coming up to the house in his brand new Fiat. He was one of the young soldiers who had been saved, and Bill had married him to an Armenian girl. When a soldier married a girl there, the American Army (or government) required an American ceremony. The Ethiopian government required a ceremony, and if the girl belonged to another church, that church required one.

Bill married one soldier to a Greek girl. We felt sorry for them when they had to endure three weddings. By the end of the festivities, they were exhausted. Bill performed the American wedding for John and Sonja at the chapel in the mission building. It was beautiful. We had all the officers and enlisted men from the base there and all of Sonja's family and friends and the missionaries. John was in full dress uniform and Sonja wore a lovely wedding dress.

Everything was just like a wedding in the States, including the frayed nerves. Bill thought we were going to lose the groom. He turned white and almost passed out during the ceremony, but Bill succeeded in pronouncing them man and wife.

John and Sonja were like part of our family, and they spent much of their free time in our home. Now, as he approached the door we knew that something was dreadfully wrong. His expression was mournful. He was in tears as he entered. He said, "Bill, I've got to talk to you. Something awful has happened."

Bill took him into his study, and John told the story. He had just gotten his new hot Fiat, and he was out on the airport road with a couple of his buddies. He was trying it out and wanted to see how fast it would go. Dumb, but typical!

His speed had reached about eighty-five miles an hour when a little Ethiopian boy, about nine years old, ran out in front of him. He still had his foot on the accelerator when he hit him. He saw him rolling in front of his car as he brought the car to a stop. He jumped out, ran to the child, put his hand under his head, and the head came off in his hand.

His hands were covered with the dried blood of that little boy and John was in anguish. Bill counseled with him from God's Word and calmed him down. He then washed the blood from his hands.

187

Because he was an American soldier and had good car insurance, he later paid three thousand American dollars to the boy's family, and the case was closed. Life was cheap in Ethiopia.

# CHAPTER 16

# *I Met the King*

~~~~~~~~~~~~~~~~~~~~~~~~~~~~~~~

*B*ill and I are very adventurous and there are plenty of experiences in Ethiopia that will live in our memories forever.

We were busy about the Lord's work and doing all that we could to win Ethiopians to Christ. In the midst of the work, we took some time out for relaxation and to attend some of the cultural events. One of the highlights of the year was the Red Cross Festival. This event was like a fair. The government allowed all of the countries to bring a lot of things into Ethiopia tax-free. Each country had a group of booths where they displayed items from their individual homeland. The things were sold, and the proceeds were donated to the Ethiopian Red Cross.

His Imperial Majesty Haile Salassie, King of Ethiopia, was the honored guest for the occasion. He had to officially open the booths before anyone could start selling. We were excited as we dressed up, camera in hand, and went to the festival. We were going to see the king! We wanted to arrive early so we could get a good picture of His Majesty. We beat the crowd and waited inside the American area.

The American Embassy had shipped in all kinds of food to sell: hot dogs, cotton candy, soft drinks, hamburgers, etc. There were different little stalls with goods from America. It was a grand occasion. Everyone was excited. We didn't have very many events that brought this much excitement. We were all waiting for the king to arrive.

It was the Ambassador's duty to escort His Majesty all around the area to see everything they had, and after he left they could start selling to the public. The ambassador's wife was not very well liked by the Americans or the Ethiopians. She was always trying to steal the show and get her picture in the paper for her own glory. As usual, she took the honor of escorting the king through the American area from her husband. She was really trying to impress him when they passed where we were standing.

He passed right next to me, so I just started walking along beside him. He was looking at everything; then he paused and looked directly at me. I seized the opportunity, quickly extended my hand to shake hands with him, and he immediately took my hand. As he held my hand, I asked him if he would permit my husband to take a picture of us. He graciously agreed.

So there we stood, posing for Bill to photograph us. Just as he snapped the picture, a man walked between us. The king waited until Bill could take another one. I bowed, thanked him, and he moved on. I had just succeeded in a great triumph! The other Americans and the Ethiopians thought I deserved applause. The Ethiopians labeled me as *gobuz* ("very brave"); I carried that title until we left Ethiopia.

However, I had not made the same impression on the ambassador's wife! I had stolen her attention. While the king was holding my hand she was unaware that he was not beside her. She continued talking and basking in the glory, until she realized what was happening. She had been talking to herself as she walked and pointed out different things to him. Suddenly, she realized that he was not by her side, but he was back with me—holding my hand for pictures! She was embarrassed, and the people were delighted. After the king left, she came to me and said, "That was not good form." (I really didn't like her form either.)

I learned later that it could have been very dangerous. His bodyguards would club anyone who tried to touch the king, but since I was next to him and quickly had my hand in his, the guards would not dare harm me. The king was then in control, and he certainly didn't seem to mind. In fact, the guards were smiling and well pleased. In their eyes I was a hero. Most of them were happy because the ambassador's wife lost the attention. I will treasure the pictures for the rest of my life.

It was a thrill to put my hand in the hand of the king of Ethiopia, but I look forward to the day when I can put my hand in the nail-scarred hand of the King of Kings, the Lord Jesus Christ.

## A Visit to the Palace Grounds

We had the opportunity to visit His Majesty's palace grounds. We were excited because there were only special times when the grounds were open to tourists. When we approached the large, lovely palace, we saw bullet holes, which were put there during an attempted coup a few years earlier. We walked behind the palace and surveyed his huge backyard. He loved animals and had given a home to many of them on these lovely grounds. The more dangerous animals were contained in large walk-in cages. We went into the cage with some beautiful cheetahs. They purred like big housecats as we petted them. One of them licked my hand. His tongue felt like sandpaper. These cats were somewhat tame but still had the potential of being fierce. Because of the ever-present threat of danger, children were not permitted to enter the cage. Wyvonna was not happy and stood outside the cage frowning.

## A Much Needed Vacation

Bill and I needed to get away from Addis for awhile. We had never visited the northern city of Asmara, where we wanted to go to live and to do a ministry. So we talked to another couple, Joe and Sue, about going on a trip to Asmara. They also needed a break from the daily strains of the work, and they agreed to go with us. They didn't have children, and the Sidebottoms, who lived on a mission station on the North road, had offered to keep our children while we went on the trip. We took Yeshi with us so she could help with them.

We arrived at the Sidebottom's house in the afternoon, spent the night, and left early the next morning. We were in our little Volkswagen bug. We put a roof rack on the car to hold our luggage. We were excited about this adventure.

Our trip would be about six hundred miles through barren mountains and unpaved roads. There was only one place where we could eat and spend the night. The little hotel belonged to an Italian, and it was about half way to Asmara. We planned to spend the night there.

We would have to travel through the mountains, where there were constant reports of road bandits. The bandits (*shiftas*) would build a blockade of large stones on the road, just around a curve. When a car would go around the curve, suddenly the driver had to stop because of the stones, and then the bandits would rob him. We had reports of them even taking the victims' clothing and vehicles. We had planned to travel only during the day because most of the robberies took place at night.

We had wonderful fun and fellowship on this trip. However, in our excitement, we had not properly planned and did not take much food with us (live and learn). We had driven all day and were getting very hungry. Surely we would arrive at the hotel soon. It was getting dark, and we didn't feel good about traveling on that road after dark.

I must admit, I was scared. My imagination took control, and I thought I could see a blockade around every curve. I have a touch of night blindness anyway, and I was straining my eyes, looking at the road. We would go around a curve, and I would say, "Bill, look out!" I thought for sure I saw something.

He finally said, "Will you stop? You are getting on my nerves. There are no blockades and everything will be fine." (When did he get so smart?)

Joe was hungry—I mean, *really hungry*! He became silent and was just bouncing along in the backseat with Sue and saying nothing. He was too hungry to talk. He was, by nature, a quiet, easygoing person. But he was quieter than usual now. He was starving!

We were wondering how much farther we had to go to get to this hotel. Even Bill was becoming a bit uneasy since it was after dark. Suddenly, the car hit a big stone in the road. It was only one so we didn't feel that it was put there deliberately. However, it was a bit spooky to have to get out of the car at this point. Bill was afraid that it might have damaged something underneath the car, so they got out and checked. It was OK. We thanked the Lord, drew a breath of relief, and drove on.

We had driven a short distance down the road, when, suddenly, Bill hit the brakes and dodged, but, too late. We hit a bigger stone that time. It jolted the car enough that it knocked our luggage rack down on the hood.

Now, we had to get out to fix the rack and put it back in position. I could see visions of bandits everywhere! Again, we were worried about the damage underneath the car. It would not have been good to be stranded on that road at night. But they put the rack back on, and everything else seemed OK, so we drove on.

## Joe Was Very Hungry

It was getting late when we finally saw the little Italian hotel up ahead. We were very relieved, and Joe knew that now he could satisfy his hunger pangs. We went in, rented a room, and settled in before going to the little dining room. By this time, we were all so hungry that we would have eaten anything that stayed still long enough.

We went to a table, sat down, looked at the menu, and ordered our food. Joe looked around and saw a big jar of instant Maxwell House coffee sitting on a little table over by the wall. It was unusual to see that kind of coffee in Ethiopia.

"Hey, waiter, bring me that coffee."

"Sir, I am not allowed to let you have any of that coffee."

"What do you mean? The coffee is here in the restaurant, and I am in here to eat, and I want some of that coffee. Now get it over here," he ordered and snapped his fingers.

The Ethiopian looked scared and finally brought him the coffee. We were all enjoying a cup of that good American Maxwell House coffee when the Italian woman noticed that we had the coffee. She looked displeased and promptly came to the table and snatched it. Then she went over and jumped all over the waiter for giving us the coffee.

Poor thing! He was afraid to give it to us and afraid not to give it to us. We learned later that it belonged to some American soldiers in that area. They just left it there so they could use it when they came in to eat. That's why the woman didn't want us to have it. It wasn't her coffee.

Joe continued shouting demands to the waiter, "Get that food over here right now." This action was so uncharacteristic for him. He never talked to people that way. Hunger had done a strange thing to him. I had known him a long time and he had never acted so rudely. Bill and I were laughing, but his wife was appalled. "Joe, what's wrong with you? I have never seen you act like this." And she started crying.

Joe said, "If you're going to cry, go to your room" as he swung his arm toward the stairs.

We ate a good meal, went to bed, had a good night's rest, and wondered how Joe was going to be the next morning. We met them for breakfast, and he was the same nice, quiet, loveable fellow that we had known so long. We realized that we had to keep some food around or it could be dangerous!

## Asmara Was Like an Oasis

We arrived in Asmara, checked into a hotel, and then went to look over the town. There was a large American military base there named Kagnew Station. It was a strategic satellite base for that part of the world. They had personnel of Navy, Army, and Air Force stationed there. We met one of the non-commissioned officers, and he invited us to their club. He helped us to get passes to go on the base and we were thrilled.

It was like Little America. They had miniature golf, bowling, and snack bars with hamburgers, hot dogs, and cartons of American candy bars! We were like kids at Christmas. We had not seen anything like this since leaving the States. These people had transported America to Ethiopia.

## The Food Was Great

That night we went to the enlisted club to eat. It was a beautiful, luxurious restaurant! There were carpets on the floors and linen tablecloths on the tables. It was difficult to imagine that we were in Africa. We must have looked like country bumpkins in the city for the first time.

All of the food was imported from the States, so we knew that it was safe. We felt that the steaks would be good, and that's what we ordered. They were delicious.

The American hostess came to our table and asked if everything was OK. We must have shocked her by raving about how wonderful everything was. She was used to dealing with the military people who took it for granted, and she probably expected complaints.

We later met some of the officers, and they invited us to their club. We ate on the base all that week. It was great! Joe was enjoying the food so much that he was oblivious to the surroundings. We went into one of the clubs to eat early in the evening. Just before we finished our meal, a band sat up and started playing music. Others got up and started dancing very near our table. Joe wanted dessert, but we felt uncomfortable, so we convinced him to leave and get dessert at the snack bar. After we got outside, he was grumbling, "Why didn't you want to have dessert in there?" Sue said, "Well, Joe, we didn't feel comfortable with those people dancing." "I didn't see anyone dancing." Joe replied. He was absorbed in the food.

We made a dumb mistake of inquiring about a hotel from a young soldier. We found the hotel and rented rooms. The first night was OK, but the next night was Friday. In our ignorance, we had chosen a hotel where a lot of the service men visited—with their Ethiopian girlfriends. Many of them had the same girlfriend, and that's all that I will say about that! That was the first time that I have been ashamed to be an American, but I was so embarrassed for America—and myself. We left the next day and went to another place to stay.

## Green Island

We took a short trip down to the coastal town of Masawa. We were permitted to eat at a small US military installation where we met a soldier who told us about a place called Green Island. It was a pretty little island where no one lived. All that was on the island was the shell of an abandoned church. They said that we could rent a boat, take a lunch, and spend a pleasant, relaxing afternoon.

We thought that it sounded like a good idea, so the cook at the center packed us a nice picnic lunch, we rented the boat, and began our adventure. It was great on the way out—until it started raining. It poured! We were soaking wet by the time we got to the island. From the looks of the sky, the rain was not going to stop for a long time. There was no shelter, only the ruins of the old church. So we quickly decided to go back to shore—all except Joe!

"I came out here to spend the afternoon, and I'm going to spend the afternoon," he said. (He was quiet but stubborn.) Sue tried to convince him to return with us, but he was adamant. He was staying.

We went back to the center and had some hot coffee as we dried out. Sue was worried all the time about Joe being out there in the rain. Finally the rain stopped. We got the boat and went back to get him.

When we got to the island, we discovered that he had made friends with an Ethiopian who was doing some repair work on the old church. They had built a fire, shared Jim's lunch, and he dried his clothes. He had thoroughly enjoyed his afternoon on Green Island.

After a wonderful week, we left Asmara and enjoyed an uneventful trip back to the Sidebottom's house. We picked up our children and Yeshi and returned to Addis. The trip had been good. We had relieved some stress and had some good laughs.

# CHAPTER 17

# The New Year Held Disappointments

Christmas was near, and we wanted to have a traditional American Christmas for the children. Again we had a problem—we needed a tree. There were no trees to purchase and most of them would not look good as a Christmas tree anyway. However, we did have a pretty decent tree growing at the side of our house. (Oh, no! Not again!) It looked nice, even though it did have to grow through the volcanic ash on the ground.

We looked at that tree for several days and tried to resist the temptation to put it in our house. Finally, the urge was too powerful and Bill cut it, right at the ground level. It looked beautiful after we decorated it, and the kids loved it. Now, don't get too critical.

The only problem was our night watchman! He was upset because Bill had refused to give him some money, so he told the landlord that Bill cut the tree. Now the Ethiopians really did not value the trees that much personally, but the landlord came with the guard to talk to Bill.

While the guard was gone, Bill covered the ground where the tree had stood with more volcanic rocks. (I know we sound very crafty and unspiritual, but I think even God understood our need for this tree—at least I hope He did.) When the guard and landlord arrived, the guard could not find the place where the tree had been, and obviously he couldn't remember. He searched everywhere but couldn't fine the stump. The landlord got angry with him for wasting his time, said a few unhappy words that we couldn't understand (we didn't want to understand either), slapped him on the head with his hat, and left.

We had an Air Force colonel in our American church who offered to let us use his American post office address, to bring in some toys for the children for Christmas. At first we refused because it was against military policy, but he and his wife insisted that the children needed toys for Christmas. We couldn't have them sent through the Ethiopian post office because we couldn't afford to pay the outrageous customs that would have been charged.

We finally accepted their kindness and ordered toys from the Sears catalog. By having them sent to his APO address, they bypassed the Ethiopian post office and customs. We had so many nice toys for them. Shaleen (who would be two that February) enjoyed ripping the paper off the packages more than the toys. When she opened the last one, she looked at me and said, "Mo, Mommy."

We had a wonderful Christmas that year. The Sidebottoms, Powells, and some of the military friends shared the day with us. We had a wonderful dinner and later sang carols and gave testimonies. The fellowship was so enjoyable and very uplifting.

We were enjoying our home, and Bill was busy in the African and American churches. People were being saved, and we continued to baptize in the makeshift baptismal tank in our garage.

The children were doing well. Greg was such a good baby. He never cried much and was very little trouble. He was healthy and eating six soft-scrambled eggs and grits for breakfast. The girls were little angels, and we had a lot of fun together.

Wyvonna loved Greg and tried to play with him the way her daddy played with her. Bill would pretend to be "eating her up" as he nibbled on her toes and stomach. She would squeal with delight. One day she went into the nursery and was looking at Greg, who was sleeping in his crib. Suddenly, I heard him screaming, which was very unusual. I ran to the room. Wyvonna stood a few feet from the bed. Her eyes were as large as saucers because Greg was crying.

I quickly picked him up to see what was wrong. I noticed little teeth marks on his little toe. It seemed that his foot happened to be outside of the railing and Wyvonna was going to "eat him up" the way Daddy did her, only she didn't know how to pretend.

One day Shaleen came crying to me, and I asked her what was wrong. "Wyvonna 'ainged' me," she sobbed. Upon checking, I found teeth prints on her arm. Bill always made this sound when he was playing with them. To Shaleen it sounded like "aing." Wyvonna was again copying her daddy.

Now, who do you think deserved the scolding—two-year-old Wyvonna or Daddy? I felt the same way.

## I Went Back into the Hospital

My health was not improving. I was still having problems with the old infection, so I entered the hospital in February for a hysterectomy. It had been one year since the conflict between the doctors about the surgery and at that time it had to be postponed. This time there was no problem and the surgery went fine under the skilled hand of Dr. Zimmerman. I remained in the hospital for about ten days. I had very good care but was so thankful that I was not an Adventist. I longed for some "real" meat. I just wasn't satisfied with their vegetarian diet.

I was disappointed that I had to be in the hospital when Queen Elizabeth visited Addis. Bill and some of our friends went to see her in the official parade. I felt that I was missing too much by being in the hospital.

## A Public Hanging

Richard and Darlene came into Addis from their station, about two hours outside of Addis. They went by, picked Bill up, and they were on the way to the hospital to visit me. While en route they noticed a large crowd of people, so they stopped to see what was happening. To their surprise, a man and woman were hanging by their necks from a tree. They had been executed for murder.

Darlene took some pictures, and a policeman saw her. When he realized what she had done, he quickly demanded the film from her camera. She argued with him because it was a new roll of film (and, of course, she didn't want to give up her good pictures of the hanging).

Richard said, "Give him the film. Here you are worrying about a roll of film, and those two people are hanging in that tree!" Darlene reluctantly took the film out of the camera and gave it to him.

The kids at the American school two blocks away said that they could hear the victims screaming until they died. It was gruesome, but the couple had robbed and murdered an Ethiopian official by bashing his head in with stones. So they really got their just punishment.

Many countries administer capital punishment in ways that shock Americans, but as a result, their crime rate is not nearly as high as in America. Nor do they spend billions of dollars in housing and feeding prisoners. They make a public example of them.

They all came to the hospital and told me about it. I was annoyed at the thought of missing all the excitement while I was confined to a hospital bed.

## Problems Bring Change

We were adjusting to the country and culture, but problems were brewing in this New Year. We were experiencing a lot of turmoil in our mission. We had been trained to be independent and to be led by the Holy Spirit of God on the mission field. However, Ethiopia was a new field and some unique policies had been put into effect for this field that were previously unknown to the principles and practices of our mission.

When our mission director was trying to open the field, he became acquainted with Mr. Able, who had been a field director for many years in another mission in Ethiopia. He knew the country, the people, and His Majesty Haile Selassie. He had arranged a meeting for our mission director and the king, which led to the opening of Ethiopia for our mission.

In his genuine zeal to get many missionaries into Ethiopia, our mission director invited Mr. Able to join our mission. Because of his knowledge of the country, they covertly agreed that Mr. Able would be the field director over all of us.

I am quite sure that both of these old, faithful servants had good intentions. But Mr. Able's training and ways were different, and he was getting a bit old for the job. (We later learned that he had been released from his position in his other mission because of some irresponsible decisions.) The missionaries going to Ethiopia were not informed of this new policy, and the pastors in our fellowship trusted the mission director because he had long years of experience and credibility.

We had been trained to believe that we were accountable to our home pastor, supporting pastors, and the missions committee that had approved us. The men had been trained to pray about where God would have them to start a church on the foreign field and then go to that location. However, in this new situation, the field director was assigning missionaries to the areas of his choosing. I know that many missions operate in this manner, but ours did not.

The country had been open for two years when we arrived, and we walked into a seething, volcanic environment, of which we were totally ignorant. The missionaries were frustrated and angry but had controlled their feelings. However, it was obvious that an explosion was inevitable.

Long before we had arrived in Ethiopia, Bill had felt that God was leading him to Asmara, which was located approximately eight hundred miles north of Addis Ababa. However, when he expressed his burden for that city, the field director told him that he couldn't go there. He had already chosen the area where he would send us.

I will not go into detail about the conflict because it would bring up old wounds and hurts. It might also damage our relationship with some of the people who were involved. I don't feel that it is in good taste to expose all of the mistakes that inflicted personal hurt to so many missionaries. Some of the pastors in America who were involved reacted in ignorance to the real situation. Much later many of them realized and admitted that they were wrong. They were good men—just misinformed. I also have no intention of discrediting these good men.

We still appreciate the dedicated lives and labor of the godly men involved. After growing more in the Lord, we understand that all men make mistakes. Being human, we were all guilty of error, but we have learned to give God the glory, in spite of everything. We must still accept (Romans 8:28), "And we know that all things work together for good to them that love God, to them who are the called according to his purpose." A lot of good came out of the bad situation.

Several missionaries were forced from the field during this time, and we were among them. Bill resigned on the field because he could not agree scripturally with the rules that were being forced upon us. He felt that the decision to resign was the right one. Some missionaries left before us and some left afterwards.

Later, the whole unfortunate affair was handled by the mission back in the States but too late for some of us. Our lives and ministries had been painfully disrupted. We felt that we, along with others, had been treated unfairly. It appeared that we had been sacrificed in order to establish a new policy and to cover the actions of others. We were hurt and disappointed in the men who had trained us. That hurt was to last for a very long time, but eventually God helped us to put it in the past. However, after the truth was revealed, the mission director and the field director resigned, and the policy was scraped.

## We Had to Say Goodbye to Ethiopia

We sold all of our furniture and many of our personal things. We packed and shipped the rest of our things to America. Six weeks after my hysterectomy, we, along with the Powells, said goodbye to friends and boarded a plane bound for the United States. Our hearts were heavy and our minds confused as we left Ethiopia, where we had prepared to spend the rest of our lives.

Mr. Able had previously told Bill, "This is the price you pay for being independent." We certainly paid a big price for the freedom to follow the Holy Spirit. We were trying to practice the teachings of the Bible and follow our training from college.

Yeshi accompanied us to the plane and cried, "Oh, my babies. You are taking them so far away." She had grown to love the children and they loved her. Unfortunately, we never saw Yeshi again, but we will see her in Heaven.

## We Visited the Holy Land

We decided to take advantage of our purchased air miles and to see some different countries en route to the States. Accompanied by the Powells, we spent two days in the Holy Land. It was difficult to be a tourist with three small children, but we made the best of it. Greg was only one year old, and we took turns carrying him. I had ordered harnesses for the girls that fit around their waists and chests, with a leash about four feet long. We had some terrible looks from the Europeans. They almost made me feel like a child abuser, but then I snapped back into reality. I realized that it was better than to let one of them run in front of a car and be killed. It's a hard job to carry an infant and control two toddlers at the same time—plus take pictures!

We walked the "Way of the Cross" and viewed the hill with the skull where they crucified my Lord. I experienced an awesome feeling as we stood inside the Garden Tomb and looked at the place where they laid Him. I could mentally see Him rising, folding His grave clothes, and emerging from that stony enclosure as the angels rolled the huge round stone from the entrance.

We went to Bethlehem where Jesus was born. We traveled to the Dead Sea and saw the caves where the Dead Sea Scrolls were found. When we viewed the remains of Jericho, I was reminded again of the marvelous miracles that God did and will perform, if we just obey Him. We also saw the place where the Good Samaritan had taken the wounded man. All of those places made the Bible so much more real to me.

I felt so privileged to see all of the places where our Lord had lived and ministered, even though my heart still hurt from our departure from Ethiopia. I was thankful that Jesus had come to die for me, and that He had given me the opportunity to view His earthly home place.

## Athens

We said goodbye to the Powells and flew to Athens, Greece. We stayed only two days, but we had the opportunity to take a tour of the Acropolis. As we were walking up Mars Hill, I paused to try to visualize the apostle Paul as he preached Christ to the Athenians. I could almost see and hear him as we stood on top of the hill. We proceeded on to the top of the Acropolis, which is a 500-foot limestone hill, looming up in the midst of the city of Athens.

We were with a tour group, and we received some of the strangest looks from the other tourists. I am sure they were wondering what kind of idiots we were. We were dressed in suits, carrying an infant, and leading two little girls in harnesses as we walked through the rocks and ancient ruins on the Acropolis.

We stood in front of the ruins of the Parthenon, that great building of architectural genius, which has been there since 438 years before Christ. I knew that the apostle Paul had once looked upon the splendor of this magnificent building. I could hardly believe that I was standing in such a historic spot. I was awed by the huge round pillars and wondered about the construction so long ago. We think that we have the best engineering in history, but I realized that to erect such a building, they must have had special intelligence and skill.

While my mind was lost in wonder my daughters brought me back to reality by telling me they had to go to the bathroom. I turned, looked around that rocky hill and thought, "It never fails. They always have to go at the most inconvenient times."

In order to get them away from the eyes of all the tourists, I headed toward some ruins a few feet from the slope of the hill. I waited until Wyvonna was finished and then instructed her, "Stand right here and don't move away from me while I help Shaleen."

After Shaleen finished, I turned to get Wyvonna. I felt a few more hairs turning white! She was standing at the edge of the hill, looking down at the city. This was a steep dropoff that would be equal to falling from a thirty-story building. I quickly grabbed her and went back to Bill and the rest of the group.

After all the stress before leaving Ethiopia and still recuperating from my surgery, I looked like death on toast. I have the proof in some pictures that a professional photographer took as we walked around through the ruins of that ancient monument. We were wondering why he kept taking pictures of everyone. We were ignorant, due to being new and naive tourists.

After we left the Acropolis, our tour bus took us to an old, historical cathedral. Bill and I were both tired and had no interest in seeing the church, so we remained on the bus. During this time, the photographer reappeared. In this short time, he had already developed the pictures and caught up with the tour to sell his souvenirs.

He came onto the bus and handed us the pictures. While we were looking at the nice five-by-seven photos the rest of the people started coming out of the church. The man ran toward the door of the bus. Bill called to him to say that we didn't want to buy the pictures. He ignored us and ran in pursuit of the other tourists. He was still doing business as the driver got on the bus, ordered everyone to board, and the bus took off. We were left holding the pictures that we never had the chance to return.

I felt blessed that this "Arkansas Traveler" had been fortunate to see a small part of Athens.

## Holland

Our next stop was Amsterdam. We arrived at the airport without reservations in a hotel. We approached an information desk and asked for assistance in finding a place to stay. (See how naive we were?)

The girl told us that it would be almost impossible to find a vacancy because there was some special event in the city and everything was filled. She finally felt sorry for us and called a few private guesthouses. She secured a room for us in a bed and breakfast. We took a taxi to the place, and we were not disappointed.

The people who owned the small hotel spoke some English and were very kind to us. We had a nice room, and the breakfast the next morning was something to behold! It was a typical Dutch meal, with several kinds of cheeses, bread, butter, eggs, and jams. We thoroughly enjoyed it before setting out on our next adventure.

We went downtown and took a boat ride on the canal. It was very enjoyable, as the driver pointed out places of interest. He showed us where Anne Frank had lived in hiding until the Germans took her prisoner. Also, he pointed to a house along the edge of the canal. He said that many years ago a butler told his wealthy boss that he would love to have a house as wide as his front door. His desire was granted. His boss built him the house, which is now known as the "narrowest house in the world."

After the canal ride, we took a tour bus out to visit Kukenhoff, where there were many acres of beautiful flowers. Every flower in Holland was displayed in abundance. During our journey, we saw the tulip fields that were in full bloom. The sights were breathtaking, miles of beautiful tulips and hyacinths. The hyacinths had a luscious fragrance that filled the air.

## London

We left Holland and arrived in London, England. Our travel agent in Ethiopia had arranged a reservation for us at a hotel in Piccadilly Circus. We took a taxi to the hotel. We were thankful to have such a nice place to stay and advance reservations.

We entered the door with our three tired children. Our eyes quickly scanned the beautiful and very expensive-looking lobby. I had never been in such an elegant place and wondered how this could be a class B hotel. I just thought that prices must be very reasonable in London. (Was I ignorant or what?)

We approached the reception desk, and to our surprise and total disappointment, they had never heard of the Cunninghams. (And we had trusted our travel agent!) We argued that the agent had made the reservation, and finally the desk clerk called the manager.

The manager came and observed us as he was informed of the situation. He was very kind and told us that, even though we did not have a reservation, he had a two-room suite that he would let us have for the price of a single room. We asked him the cost, and we were shocked at the high price (which I don't remember). We thanked him for his kindness but told him that we couldn't afford to stay there. We would have to look for another hotel. We were really like country bumpkins in the big city.

We certainly couldn't disguise our ignorance, and evidently he felt sorry for us. He explained that it would cost much more money for a taxi to take us to look for another hotel. I am sure that we looked very pitiful. He quickly said that he would help us because we were foreigners with little children. Thank God for that kind Englishman. He gave us that beautiful suite, which overlooked the square of Piccadilly Circus, for a very reasonable amount. We were so grateful.

We were very hungry, so about seven o'clock, we inquired about the location of the dining room. We anticipated splurging on a nice meal. A stiff-lipped English waiter met us at the door. He was wearing a black suit and had a white tea towel draped over his arm. (We were walking in tall cotton!) He didn't make us feel very welcome as he glared at our children. He grudgingly took us to a table and seated us. We asked him for a highchair for Greg and this seemed to disturb him even more. It didn't take a rocket scientist to interpret his strong body language—children were not welcome in the dining room.

We had been afraid to drink the water until we arrived there. We felt that the water in London was surely safe, so we ordered water along with our meal. The waiter brought us a pitcher of the most tantalizing ice water my eyes have ever had the privilege to look upon. We drank it instantly and asked for more. (We weren't making friends and influencing waiters at this point.) We drank so many pitchers of that delicious water that it would have embarrassed the ordinary person, but missionaries aren't ordinary. Each time we ordered we received that irritated side-glance from the completely British waiter. Most of the people were staring at us as if we should not be in the dining room. We wondered why because, after all, we were staying in the hotel, and we were dressed acceptably.

We weren't like the missionaries from Africa that I heard about. They were going to America for a furlough after four years on the mission field. They ordered new clothing from Sears so they would look nice when they arrived in America. They couldn't understand why everyone was staring at them and laughing when they arrived at Kennedy Airport. They finally understood when they turned to check on their kids, who were following them, carrying their suitcases on their heads!

We saw that the waiters were very nervous and acted like the children were going to mess up their beautiful thick carpet. We noticed there were no other children in the dining room. We finished our very delicious meal and went to our room.

We have laughed about that night so many times. We learned much later that in the British culture, the children are fed early and put to bed. They never have the dinner meal with the parents, especially in a swank hotel dining room!

## We Missed Our Flight

Our plane from London to New York was late in arriving, so we missed our connecting flight to go on to Ohio, where Bill's family lived. We had to sit in the airport in New York about seven hours. The kids were very tired from the long flight. However, they had shifted into the activity that accompanies boredom and exhaustion. I usually made them sit still and behave, but Bill and I were so tired. We watched as they rolled and played on the terminal floor. If I had been in my right mind, I would have thought about all the germs on the floor, but I just sat in a daze and watched them.

When we finally arrived in our home airport in the wee hours of the morning, there was no one to meet us. We had to hire the airport limousine service to take us home. Later, we learned that the family and church had staged a grand welcoming party for us at the airport. But they had gone home in disappointment while the kids were polishing the floor in the New York airport.

The family was happy to see us, and we were so relieved to be home. I knew that all the stress definitely had a positive advantage when my mother-in-law took one look at me and asked, "Are you sick?"

I had lost a lot of weight, and I realized, to my great joy, that everything was not in vain.

# CHAPTER 18

# No Home, No Money, and No Job

We didn't know what we were going to do. Our financial support was canceled upon our arrival in the States, and we had no place to live. We were forced to stay with Bill's parents until we could get settled.

The five of us slept in the basement of his parents' home. His mom put five temporary beds in the large furnace room that was to be our home for the next four months! We didn't like the idea of having to depend on, or impose upon, the kindness of his parents, but we had no choice.

We were able to purchase a new car with the money that we had acquired from the sale of our car and all of our belongings in Africa. We ordered a new Pontiac before we left Ethiopia, from a wholesale dealer in Detroit.

We borrowed a car from Bill's cousin and drove to Detroit to get our new Pontiac Tempest. I was thankful later and realized Bill's wisdom in forcing me to drive the new car out of Detroit. However, at the time I was scared to death, and he wasn't my favorite person. I had not driven while we were in Africa, and I was not prepared to reacquaint myself with the art in the middle of Detroit. I begged him to let me drive the old car. I would rather wreck it. But he insisted that I drive the new one. I didn't like him for a short time!

We shipped some of our personal things back from Ethiopia, and we were notified that they had arrived on the East Coast. We had to be peeled off the ceiling when we were informed that we had to pay a shipping bill before we could receive them. We had prepaid the bill before we left Ethiopia, but it seemed that the shipper had ripped us off and sent the things "to be paid on delivery." You might know! Education is expensive. We should never have trusted that shipping agent.

The Powells were staying at his brother's house in Rhode Island, so we drove up to meet them, and together we were going to claim our shipments. (They had used the same shipping company, and had been ripped off too.)

Delmar knew the area, so we let him drive his new car. (Remember that we had all been used to hazardous, mountainous dirt roads in Ethiopia. Now here we were trying to adjust to the huge frightening American interstates.)

The Powells were both in the front seat, and Bill and I were in the back with their son. We were talking and trying to comfort each other in our misery and disappointment as we cruised down the highway. Helen was sitting sideways and had her head turned to us while talking. She turned her head to the front just as Delmar was changing from the left lane to the right lane. She quickly noticed that the car was going toward the other side of the road. We suddenly heard the most blood-curdling scream as she yelled, "Delmar, look out!"

Bill stills swears that the hair stood out straight on the back of Delmar's neck. He turned white as he responded in a terrified voice, "What's wrong?" He thought she had seen something that he didn't see. He managed to keep the car under control through the panic. By this time, he somewhat rudely informed Helen that he was only changing lanes, but she thought he was running off the road toward some trees.

After the shock, Delmar was mad, Helen was embarrassed, and Bill and I were laughing hysterically in the back seat (which didn't really help Delmar's disposition).

We finally managed to clear our shipments—after paying the bill again—and arranged to have our things delivered to Ohio.

We stayed a couple of nights with the Powells in the home of his brother and enjoyed some good fellowship and hospitality. His brother was a very dignified artist, and he was in no small way surprised and appalled at the uncouthness of these African missionaries.

We were used to seeing life in the raw. I'm afraid that we didn't have much refinement in describing some of the things that we had experienced in Africa. We were accustomed to the things that we saw in Ethiopia, but the description seemed crude back in America. His brother lovingly (I think) suggested that there should be some kind of classes to help us to get reoriented to the American lifestyle. We had not realized that we had lost so much of our culture!

## They Begged Us to Come to Chicago

One of the military couples who had come to Christ through our ministry in Ethiopia was now living in Chicago. They begged us to come there to start a church. We left our children with Bill's parents and drove there, to see if it would be God's will for us to minister in that city.

We arrived in time to be able to comfort this family during a family tragedy. Her brother had crashed in a helicopter, had barely escaped death, and was critical. We thought, "Well, maybe this is where the Lord wants us."

We chose the area where we would start a church, and Bill had been accepted in a management-training program at a fast food restaurant. Then his mother called and said that his home pastor, Dr. Harold Henniger, had promised to put him on full financial support if he would come back to Ohio and accept the pastorate of a small church in a nearby town.

## Bill Suffered from Malaria

After much prayer, Bill decided to take his pastor's advice and support. So we returned to Ohio. He accepted the call to the pastorate of the small church, and we were trying to locate a house in the area when Bill started to get sick. For three days he had high fever and chills. When the chills came, he shook so hard that I thought he would break the chair where he was sitting.

I begged him to go to the doctor but he refused. He insisted that it was nothing serious and that he would be OK. Malaria was very prevalent in Ethiopia. In fact, Bill had gone to the doctor while we were there with some of the same symptoms. They gave him the malaria treatment and he got better. Now, I was almost sure that he had malaria. Finally, I could stand it no longer. I called his brother-in-law, who was a doctor.

"Sam, I need to bring Bill in for you to check him. Can you see him this afternoon?"

"What's seems to be wrong with him?"

"He has chills and high fever. I think he has malaria. Please let me bring him in."

He had a slight panic in his voice as he said, "I have never treated a case of malaria. I don't know anything about it."

"Well, who can I call? Please recommend someone who can help him."

He gave me the names of five doctors, and I called four of them before I could get anyone who was willing to even look at him. Of course, I suppose they wondered what kind of a horrible, contagious African disease could be living in his body that might jeopardize the whole city.

Finally, I called the last doctor on the list, Dr. Bucher, who was from Bulgaria. I explained the case to him and asked if I could bring him in for treatment. (If this had occurred in Ethiopia, the doctors would have calmly given him quinine medication, and it would have been no big thing.)

Dr. Bucher said, "I haven't even seen a case of malaria in ten years, but bring him in, and I will check him."

As soon as he looked at Bill, he started making arrangements to admit him to the hospital. I thought, "Wonderful, within a few hours he will get some comfort." *Wrong!*

He agonized and endured four days of experimentation in the hospital. His fever would rise to 107 degrees, and he would be delirious. He would pull the back of his head and neck up onto the cold metal headboard of the bed to try to get some relief. His mouth was covered with fever blisters.

I think every doctor in that city came into his room. They would stand just inside the door to look at the case of the decade. They seemed afraid to venture up to the bed. Every time he had a chill, the nurses would run in and draw blood. They took so much blood; they should have paid us for it.

My temper cannot be subdued indefinitely. Finally, I lost it! I pounced on the doctor. "When are you going to start treating him? He is suffering needlessly."

"Well, we must be sure it is malaria, so we are taking blood samples during the chills when it is active in the blood stream."

I came off center. "You know it's malaria, and I know its malaria. And I know you are just using him for a guinea pig. You get some quinine into him right now, or I'm going to remove him from this hospital and take him somewhere where I can get some help!" The strain of his sickness and the responsibility of trying to bridge the gap between him and the new church was beginning to show on me.

I think he knew that the classes were over! He immediately started treatment. Within a few hours the symptoms were diminishing, and he was beginning to feel a little better. The malaria left him anemic, and he craved tomato juice, which I took to him each time I visited. He couldn't seem to get enough of the juice to satisfy him. He stayed in the hospital a few more days and finally felt strong enough to go home.

## We Finally Moved into Our Own Home

Even though Bill's parents had been very good to us during the four months we had stayed with them, I was elated to move into our own little house and to have my own furniture. We were able to get a nice, little three-bedroom house with a full basement, where the kids could play without the risk of danger. (I was always paranoid that something would happen to one of them and would not let them out of my sight.)

We borrowed money to put a chain link fence around the backyard so they could play outside. Bill's mom bought them a nice swing set, and it was such a pleasant change from having them play in our African volcanic rock-covered yard.

One day I went out to check on the girls and they were gone! I almost panicked! Had someone stolen them out of the yard? I ran outside, started looking in both directions and saw them at the end of the block. I ran to where they were and was stunned to see them both standing over a big open pipe that went down into a well. I still cannot understand why it was there—or open. That was during the time in the late sixties when so many children were killed by falling down open well pipes.

I yanked them back to the house, spanked them soundly for climbing over the fence and *escaping* from the yard, and put them to bed. I still feel a little guilty for spanking them, but I was so frightened at the possibility of one of them falling down that pipe that I acted a lot out of fear. But they were also spanked for climbing over the fence. I had never even considered that they would do that. (Oh, no! Did they inherit my adventuresome spirit?)

We worked hard to build that little church. Bill made one hundred house calls every week. The church started to grow. Bill took the church when the attendance was about twenty people. Within a year, we had over one hundred people. Then, Delmar Powell came by to visit us.

Our minds were still on the mission field, and the more he talked, the more the Lord fingered around our hearts. He told us that the mission had cleared up most of the problems in Ethiopia, and the board was trying to contact us. They wanted us to be reinstated and return to the field. However, the wounds were still too fresh. I know that it is not the spiritual thing to bear grudges or to let bitterness grow in your heart, and we were sinning a little in both areas.

However, John and Gail, who had left Ethiopia shortly before we had left, had been approved by another mission and returned to Ethiopia. We talked to a pastor who was associated with that mission, and he encouraged us to seek their approval. We then phoned the director of the mission. He told us that they were having a meeting soon and invited us to attend.

We were approved by the World Baptist Fellowship Mission exactly one year after taking the church. Bill resigned as pastor, and we started making plans to return to Ethiopia.

# CHAPTER 19

# On the Road Again

We had to raise our support all over again, which would take at least one year of traveling. Since the children were not in school yet, we wanted our family to be together. (Wyvonna would be starting to school upon our arrival in Ethiopia.) We bought a seventeen-foot camper trailer, sold our furniture and house, and started back on the road. The new fellowship of churches welcomed us. We had no problem in raising our support and the needed equipment to get us to the field. However, deputation always offers many experiences and challenges. This year was no different.

## Chicken Pox

We parked our trailer just outside the church during a mission conference in West Texas. While I was getting the children ready for church I noticed some red spots on Wyvonna. Bites? No, they had the appearance of—chicken pox! "Oh, Lord, this is not the best time."

But timing is not always perfect, and all three of them broke out with the chicken pox that week. Some of the women of the church took turns relieving me while I participated in the conference. One of them was a nurse. She advised me to get a surgical soap and wash them in it. I heeded her advice and it worked wonders. The pox dried up and the kids experienced very minimal misery. They were all so good during that time.

One night during this stressful week I was hurrying to get ready for church. I grabbed the spray and quickly sprayed my hair. I stared and gasped! I had used my powdered deodorant instead of the hairspray. And that was in the time when highlights were not in fashion.

## Bees and More Bees

We were in Pittsburgh for a meeting with old friends from college. Janet had been matron of honor in our wedding and Billy was our soloist. They had gone there and built a very successful church, where Bill was scheduled to preach during our visit. We were looking forward to good fellowship with them.

The men were on visitation and Janet and I were in the backyard with Wyvonna and Shaleen. It was in the fall of the year, and the weather was still nice. We were visiting while the girls were digging in the dirt in a small knoll behind the house. Suddenly they screamed. Janet and I ran to them and were horrified to see bees all over them. They had dug into a nest of yellow jackets that had gone underground for the coming winter. Wyvonna was closest to the nest and the whole swarm came after her. Shaleen had only a few on her. Janet grabbed her and ran in one direction, and I ran toward the house with Wyvonna. I ran into the house and closed the door, which blocked out the majority of the swarm.

The bees were matted in Wyvonna's hair, and I pulled them out one by one with my fingers. I received a few stings in the process, but her face and head were covered with stings. After the bees were gone, Janet brought Shaleen into the house, and we put damp baking soda on their stings. The baking soda soothed them and prevented a lot of discomfort. We called a doctor and were told that medical treatment would not be necessary, unless they experienced different reactions.

## The Children's Home Was the Car

As I look back, I marvel at how well they adjusted to the traveling and the incidents along the way. They were brave little soldiers. Many times the car was their bedroom. Two of them would sleep on the seat and one on the floor until we could find a place to park the trailer for the night. They were exceptional children under the circumstances.

Bill and I were quiet as the car moved down the highway. I could hear the children talking and playing in the back seat. They were playing church. No wonder! I let my mind relax and drift, until I heard Wyvonna getting a little annoyed.

I turned to see what the problem was. She had Greg down on his knees by the seat and was telling him how to accept Jesus as his Savior. I listened as she quoted all the needed scriptures to him and explained the procedure very well. But when three-year-old Greg refused to cooperate, she lost her patience, and she called to me, "Mom, Greg won't let me save him!" She had gotten a little confused about her job.

## I Learned About a West Texas Blizzard

One Sunday evening we had just finished a mission conference in West Texas. At church that night the people were talking about a blizzard that was due to hit the area the next day. I laughed to myself thinking, "This is West Texas. Why are they so fearful of what they call a blizzard? They should have been raised in Michigan."

The next morning we pulled up stakes and left for our next conference, which was starting on Wednesday night in Savannah, Georgia. I soon learned about a West Texas blizzard! I had to eat a lot of my words. It was something to dread. The snow fell and the wind blew. By the time we arrived in Ft. Worth, the other missionaries (who were going to Georgia) called and cancelled their meeting.

They begged Bill to cancel. They told him that it was too dangerous to try to drive through the bad weather. But Bill is from Ohio and had lived through many bad winters. He said, "No, I can make it. I have scheduled that conference, and I'm not going to cancel."

We were pulling the trailer with a Ford Bronco. Much of the time Bill had to drive with two wheels off the pavement to get enough traction to continue. The snow was blinding as it pounded the windshield. I had never seen anything that bad in Michigan. We rarely saw a car on the highway. Everyone was off the roads. We met one car and we almost covered it in snow as we passed.

We drove day and night and only stopped for a few hours to sleep and eat. It was a miracle that we did not lose the trailer, but we continued on toward Savannah. The blizzard was the worse in several years and extended all the way south.

## We Got Stuck on the Median

Finally, after three exhausting days of driving in those conditions, we were nearing Savannah. Bill made a wrong turn on the interstate. We had two more hours to reach the church before the meeting started. We had no idea how far we would have to go before we could turn around, but we feared the worst. Bill started across the median. There wasn't any snow, but he didn't realize that the ground was so soft. He got stuck!

We then had two problems: being late for the conference *and* getting a ticket for crossing the median. He tried to free the car, but it wouldn't budge. Desperately, he started gunning the engine. "I will burn the tires off of this thing before I get caught on this median," he fumed.

We even pushed (remember, we were pulling a trailer). Finally, I think our guardian angel gave us a hand, and we were able to get back up on the road. We thanked God for His help and headed back in the right direction.

Church started at 7:30 P.M., and we arrived in front of the building at 7:15! Bill rushed inside, and the pastor and his twelve-year-old son hurried out to help us carry our things up to a missionary apartment over the church.

Bill quickly freshened up, changed clothes, and ran downstairs to the meeting. I washed the kids the best I could and changed their clothes. I then focused my attention on trying to make myself as presentable as possible in a few minutes. That was not easy because I was a mess! I changed clothes, put on some makeup, and plopped my wig on to cover my wrecked hair. (Thank God for wigs. In those days, I carried two of them.) Hmmm, I looked pretty good—considering what I had just been through.

The kids and I went down for the service. When we were introduced, no one realized what frustration was hidden behind our masks. Missionaries have to perform a lot. We smiled and pretended that we had just stepped out of the Holiday Inn.

After the service, the pastor's son said to him in private, "Dad, what happened to that lady that we took upstairs?" Don't tell me that women should go without makeup and wigs!

That reminds me of a funny story about my wigs. We were in a mission conference in Michigan with some other missionaries. We had free time during the afternoon, so we were all sitting around in the fellowship hall. I had a bad headache and another missionary wife was massaging my neck.

"If you take your wig off, I can massage the back of your head, and maybe the headache will go away."

"OK," I said.

I just reached up and pulled the wig off. Just as I did, one of the men with whom we had shared many conferences looked my way. He almost had a stroke. He had no idea that I ever wore wigs, and it shocked him to see me take my hair off. For years after that I could never convince him that the hair he saw on my head was my own!

## I Was So Tired That the Idea of Rest Made Me Laugh

After the service, we had a good night's rest and went on to our next meeting in Atlanta. When we arrived, the pastor said the whole church had been praying for our safety.

The other missionaries had told him that Bill refused to cancel and that we were on the road in that horrible blizzard. I am sure that their prayers helped to get us there safely. I was still so tired that I was giddy.

I was scheduled to sing and I had chosen the old favorite, *Zion's Hill*. In the second verse, there was something about rest. When I sang that part, Bill loudly exclaimed, "Amen." Since I was on the verge of hysteria anyway, I got tickled. I couldn't keep my composure, so I just stood and laughed until I could gain control. The pianist continued to play (bless her.) When I regained my composure, I picked up the song and continued. Everyone laughed with me because they realized what we had just gone through.

## Our Needs Were Always Met

During that trip, we had a window broken in the trailer, but we didn't have the spare money to have it replaced. Bill put some cardboard and plastic over it until we could have it fixed. We pulled into a gas station, somewhere in Georgia, and another customer started talking to Bill. It was in the winter, and the man was curious about why we were on the road in bad weather. Bill told him that we were missionaries on our way to Africa.

He noticed the window and asked, "Why haven't you had that replaced?"

"I just haven't had the extra money," Bill replied.

"Do you have a little time now that you can spare?"

"Sure. Why?"

"I want to have a window put in there for you."

He had the window replaced, gave us twenty dollars, and wished us a good trip as we left. God always supplied our needs, even through strangers. God tells us in (Luke 6:38), "Give, and it shall be given unto you; good measure, pressed down, shaken together, and running over, shall men give unto your bosom. For with the same measure that ye mete withal it shall be measured to you again."

## The Foot Doctor

We met many different kinds of people during our years of traveling, but we will always remember the foot doctor and his family. We were in the mission conference of a large church in Ohio, and we stayed in the home of the foot doctor. They were very hospitable to us and provided a lot of entertainment. The doctor had a great dry sense of humor. The first morning we were there we were awakened at four o'clock in the morning by a loud noise outside our bedroom door. Bill jumped up and went to check. The doctor had set a blaring radio near the door and was enjoying our reaction.

Bill asked him why he had chosen to be a foot doctor. He replied, "I thought I would just start at the bottom and work up."

His elderly mother-in-law lived with them. One day, she, the doctor, and I were sitting in the sunroom, enjoying a relaxing conversation. Suddenly, she said, "Well, I wonder where my check is. It should have been here by now."

The doctor said, "There you go, worrying about that social security check. What you should be worrying about is whether people are going to Heaven or Hell." I wanted to laugh so much that I was about to burst as they continued arguing. The rebuke was funny because the doctor wasn't that concerned over the eternal destiny of people. But he didn't mean to be disrespectful to the Lord either.

Another day, we were all sitting at the dining table eating dinner when the old lady entered from one door, walked through the room, and out the other door. She didn't speak to anyone but was just saying, "The Bible says that in the end of time, you can't tell summer from winter, except by the falling of the leaves and the budding of the trees." We all looked at her as she nonchalantly moved into another room.

Their actions and sense of humor kept us laughing the whole time we were there. It was more comical because they acted so serious in all of their comments. During the week, we mentioned their strangeness to the pastor. He laughed and said, "Oh, yeah. They are killing each other in that house."

I thought, "Well, thanks a lot for putting us there."

## I Dropped My Gun in Front of the Deacons

Bill had purchased a small tear gas pistol in a leather holster for me to carry in my purse. He thought it would provide some protection if I ever needed it. It looked like a real .22 pistol.

We were in a mission conference in a large church. During a break in the meetings, I was standing in the vestibule with some other missionaries and members of the church, including some of the deacons. Groups of people had gathered and were listening to some of our missionary stories. I started to get something out of my purse and that gun fell out in the middle of the floor—before the eyes of God and everybody! You should have seen the shocked expressions on the faces of the church members. I couldn't evaporate, and I didn't feel like trying to cover it with long explanations. I just reached down, picked it up, laughed, and said, "A missionary can't even carry a gun without everyone knowing about it."

Later, I did explain that it was only a tear gas gun, and they laughed with me. Apparently, they didn't hold it against me because we did get support from that church. I am sure they remember me as "the pistol-packing missionary."

We traveled for approximately a year before we had the support that we needed to return to Ethiopia. We met many wonderful people and made many new friends, but we were ready to get back to Africa.

## Wyvonna Had a Severe Allergic Reaction

We were packing our barrels for shipping, and the children were playing outside. I ran to Wyvonna when I heard her screaming. Bumblebees had stung her! I put some medicine on the stings, calmed her down, and finished packing. A short time afterwards, we went back to Bill's parents' house and Wyvonna got sick. When she vomited, I thought she was just suffering from an upset stomach. But she continued to vomit.

I called a doctor and told him that she was continuously vomiting and asked him what I could do for her. In the course of the conversation, I told him about the bee stings. He almost came unglued.

"You get that child immediately to the emergency room. She could die. And next time don't wait this long to call a doctor." Well, excuse me, and please replace my head. After his outburst, he told me that she was allergic to bee stings, but I didn't know.

We rushed her to the hospital and she was admitted. They treated her for three days and released her. The doctor explained to me that she had a lot of the poison in her system from the previous stings in Pittsburgh and that it never leaves the body. Therefore, when she got these stings, it brought about the severe reaction. There is no way of telling how much the body can handle, and even one sting can be fatal. Since then we have been very careful. We made sure that she carried medication with her all the time. But she was never stung again.

## If It's Not Bees, It's Dogs

We were visiting with Bill's uncle and aunt during the time that we were preparing to leave. They lived on a farm where it was safe for the children to play outside unsupervised. I checked on them often, but during a time when I was in the house talking with the rest of the adults, they were alone outside.

I was going out the door to check on them when I met Wyvonna and Shaleen. They were frightened and said that the dog (an old Chow) had bitten Greg. As I ran toward the backyard, Greg (about three years old) was coming around the corner of the house. He was crying and his face was a bloody mess. I screamed and ran to him. His face was already badly swollen. We rushed him to the hospital. The doctor treated him and stitched the wounds. He healed quickly, with the exception of one wound on his cheek that became infected and was treated.

Bruno evidently went for his throat, and Greg moved enough so that the dog sank his teeth into each cheek and just about his upper lip. The authorities took the dog and kept him locked up for a few days, to check him for disease. He was OK, so they released him back to Bill's uncle.

We were so angry and felt that the dog should have been destroyed. Bruno was old and irritable, but I had never seen anything to make me think he was vicious. He was not used to being around children, so Greg may have provoked him in a playful way. Naturally, as most owners of vicious dogs do, the uncle blamed Greg. We had no idea that the dog would be dangerous around the children or we would never have permitted them to be outside with him.

I thank the Lord that Greg's face was not disfigured and the scars are unnoticeable today. When he was about fifteen years old, he wanted to play the trumpet, but the instructor said that the injury had left a weakness above his lip that prevented him from playing the horn.

It's so comforting to know that God takes care of our children when we can't protect them.

# CHAPTER 20

## *We Returned like a Moth to a Flame*

Once again we said goodbye to family and friends and boarded a plane for Ethiopia. I wasn't frightened this time because I knew what to expect (I thought). We were finally going to Asmara, the city that we felt God had called us to six years ago.

We went back by faith, trusting that we would be able to remain in the country. The communists had succeeded in getting the young people stirred up in Addis Ababa. At the same time, the Eritrea Army was preparing to wage a war of independence from Ethiopia. Eritrea was taken over by Ethiopia during the World War, and they were struggling to regain their independence. Asmara was the capital city of Eritrea.

We had to lay over in Madrid, Spain for two days. While we were there, we met a man from Australia. Bill explained to him where we were going and why. He also expressed our fear that we wouldn't be able to remain in Ethiopia, due to the threat of war there. The Australian said, "Well, mate, if you can't stay in Ethiopia, then come on down and help us."

Bill tucked that statement into his memory bank. We didn't realize how it would affect our lives in the future.

## Beirut, Lebanon

We visited some missionary friends in Lebanon for one week. We went sightseeing every day and saw so many historical places of interest. We almost ran the missionary to death. Toward the end of the week, we were climbing some steps at the biblical site of Biblos. He was so tired that he started to giggle. Finally, when he could talk, he said, "I'll be so glad when you leave so I can get some rest."

We were on our way to visit Tyre and Sidon, and we had to pass through "no man's land." We were stopped at a checkpoint. They told us that if we wanted to proceed on we would have to leave our passports there until we returned. We were still a bit ignorant, so we complied. Today no one will separate me from my passport in a foreign country.

God protected us, but the sight of machine gun nests along the road made us very uneasy. We enjoyed seeing these old historical towns where the fishermen were sitting out mending their nets. I could almost visualize the fishermen of the Bible days.

We went to visit the five remaining "Cedars of Lebanon." We left Beirut and drove up into the mountains. This was the place from where Solomon took the trees to build the temple. There were souvenir stands under the trees where they sold woodcarvings made from the cedar wood.

The trees are protected by the government, but they could use the limbs that fell from the trees.

I was bargaining with one man about an item that I wanted to buy when we noticed some other men coming down the hill. The missionary had been previously evacuated from Beirut at gunpoint and was still a bit nervous. He saw those men coming toward us and said, "Pay him now, and let's get out of here." I don't think they were going to hurt us, but we didn't argue with him. We could understand his anxiety.

We visited many excavations of old temple sites in historical places. Everywhere we went was potentially dangerous with the children because some of those excavations went down about thirty feet. Bill was always taking pictures of everything, and I had the nerve-wrecking job of watching our children, who were almost four, five, and six years old.

They were naturally curious and running around to look at everything. I couldn't keep my eyes on all three of them at one time. It frightened me when they would move too close to the excavations. I was so afraid they were going to get hurt. Finally, I got so tired that I sat down on a large boulder and called the kids to me. They came and lined up, side by side, in front of me. I proceeded to paint a horrible picture of what would happen to them if they fell down one of those places.

I said, "OK, kids, I'm tired, and I don't feel like running after you any more. I've told you and told you that you are going to fall down one of those places and hurt yourselves. But you won't listen to me, so I am going to just sit here and rest. When you fall down into those sharp rocks, they are going to cut right through your bodies, and the fall will break your legs and arms." (I was speaking from frustration.)

I can't even remember the terrible things I told them. They patiently listened until I was finished, and then, just as if they had rehearsed, they said in unison, "No Mama, because Jesus is watching over us."

For a split second, I was not excited about their faith. Instead, I felt like tossing them over myself. Then I regained enough energy to have a good laugh. After that, they were good and listened to me. Am I a rotten mother? Probably. But fatigue and fear can produce amazing reactions.

## Our Arrival in Asmara

This time I was excited and happy when our plane landed in Asmara. We got out and walked across the tarmac to the terminal. John and Gail greeted us with a welcoming party and a huge banner that said, "Cunninghams, Welcome to Asmara."

We went to stay with them until we could get a house of our own. We were so eager to be settled again in our own home after traveling for about a year and a half.

John invited Bill to work with him in the church that he had already started. He had been able to rent a nice compound with a good building. He had church services for the Ethiopians and also English services for the US military personnel who were stationed at Kagnew Station. They represented the Army, Navy, and Air Force.

Gail was a teacher and she had started a kindergarten for upper-classed Ethiopian children. I was to join her in that work.

Asmara was a pretty town, with palm trees on both sides of the main street. It had a strong Italian influence. It was smaller, much cleaner, and more pleasant than Addis Ababa was.

## God Blessed Us with a Nice House

We looked at many houses, but they were not suitable. One day, as we were driving around the city we went into an area where there were many nice ranch-style houses. They were all fenced and had small yards with grass. They even had garages. We noticed that one was empty. We inquired about it and learned that it belonged to the government. We were told who to see about it, and immediately we went to ask if it would be possible for us to rent it.

The government official took us to see the inside of the house, and to our complete surprise, the man said that we could rent it. The price of the rent was even much less than some of the other houses that we had looked at. We were elated.

The house was beautiful. It looked very much like a ranch-style house in America. It had a nice open plan. There was a large living room with a beautiful fireplace. The dining room was large and opened to the living room. The kitchen even had cabinets. There were three bedrooms, two bathrooms, and a study. We could not believe that the master bedroom had a private bath. It was really better than any of the American houses we had lived in.

However, there was one problem with the house. It was infested with cockroaches. (I suppose these were African by nationality.) We had to rid the house of these pests before we could move into it. We bought some insecticide bombs and put them in the house and then closed it for three days.

After the three days, we found thousands of dead cockroaches. We cleaned the house and thought we had solved the problem. But the next day we were discouraged to see more live ones. Upon inspecting every place that they could be breeding, Bill finally found that there was an electrical conduit with a metal cap in the kitchen. He removed the screws, took the cap off, and saw hundreds of the little pests. That was their breeding place.

He put one of the bombs into it and closed it up. When he opened it a couple of days later, they were all dead. Hooray! We had eliminated the problem and could move into our beautiful new home.

We bought some furniture from military people who were transferring back to the States, and our house was beginning to look like a home. By this time our shipment had arrived from the States, and we now had all of our personal belongings to make life more comfortable.

We were busy and really enjoying both the American and the African churches. I was helping Gail in the kindergarten. Our kids had settled into their new home and were feeling quite happy.

## Police Brutality

Bill was excited when he heard about the Grand Prix race that was going to be driven in Asmara. This was an important annual car race that was driven in the streets of the city. Most of the drivers were Italian, and their cars included the Ferrari, Porsche, Alfa Romero, Fiat Abarth, some hot Volkswagens, and others.

One of our Italian friends (Vince) had a new Alfa Romero. When he learned that Bill liked speed, he asked him to drive his Alfa in the race. Bill was ready and willing—but I wasn't. I wouldn't agree. Bill tried to convince me that nothing could go wrong. However, I reminded him that if he should accidentally kill an Ethiopian that he would never live to drive another car. The risk was too great since we were foreigners. I think the Lord finally appealed to his logic, and he resisted the temptation.

The excitement was high on the day of the race. Vince's house had a balcony overlooking the street where the race was to start and finish. He and his wife invited us to come to their place for a good view. Thousands of people lined the streets to see which car was faster and which driver would go away with the prize.

After the race was over, and the Fiat Abarth was triumphant, people started to disperse. A four-story building was across the street from where we stood, and people had gone upstairs to have a good view of the street. As we watched we saw two American women (wives of soldiers) step off the curb and call to their husbands to toss the car keys to them. An Ethiopian policeman approached them and told them to get back up on the sidewalk. Since the race was over, he had no reason for rebuking them. They were arguing when the policeman suddenly drew his black-jack and landed a blow to the head of one of the women. The impact knocked her through the plate glass window of the store building.

The husbands were almost immediately down the stairs and onto the scene. But the policeman was whisked away by other Ethiopian policemen. They knew that he would be a dead man if the angry husbands could get hold of him.

The woman was taken to the base hospital, and we were asked to go along and file a report of what we had witnessed. Thankfully, she had minor injuries. The policeman was never located, and the soldier was immediately transferred from the country.

## There Was Trouble on the Horizon

Bill and John continued to work with the government to get our permanent residence visas. They were told that they must make a trip to Addis Ababa to speak with the minister of education. It seemed that they had no choice but to travel the eight hundred miles to Addis Ababa.

I didn't like the idea of staying behind with our three small children, but we had a lot of friends in the church from Kagnew Station. They promised to assist us in any-way that we needed them. Also, Gail and I would be spending most of the time together during the week that the men would be gone.

After the men left, she and I went shopping to get some food. We sensed that something was not right in the city. There seemed to be tenseness in everyone, and they were grabbing food in the stores as if there would be no more supplies. The shelves were already almost empty.

We called an Ethiopian friend and asked what was happening. She informed us that the Eritrea Liberation Army was going to invade the city with seventy thousand troops the next day. Their intention was to capture the city from the Ethiopian Army. This was not a good situation, especially with our husbands being eight hundred miles away.

We bought all the food that we could find, in case we would not be able to leave the house for a few days. We had every reason to believe that we would see war and a lot of bloodshed. It would not be safe to be on the streets.

In the meantime, our husbands had heard what was happening in Asmara, but they were helpless to do anything. The war would start before they could ever get home, if they had left immediately. All they could do was pray and trust us to the Lord for safekeeping.

It was a scary feeling to sit in the house and just listen for the gunshots to start. We prayed a lot and trusted God to care for us. We were trying to remain calm so the children wouldn't know what grave danger lay ahead for all of us. During a time of war in Africa, it is a common thing for women to be raped, homes to be ransacked, and for people to be killed at random.

I will be forever grateful to some of the military men from the church. They took turns on their off duty hours to keep a constant watch on our house. They were armed and constantly checked in on us to assure us that they would keep us safe.

Gail came to my house to spend the night, and we tried to patiently wait through the next twenty-four hours. Our electricity went off during the night, and we knew that the plan of the Liberation Army was being carried out. They were going to hit all of the power plants and take the city during the darkness. We waited and prayed.

Morning came and everything was still calm. Later in the day, we received news that everything would be OK. The Ethiopian army had managed to successfully put down the revolt after the first power plant was attacked. Praise God for protecting us from possible destruction.

## We Had Three Days to Leave Ethiopia

Seven months after our arrival in Asmara, Bill again went to the visa office, hoping that they would give us the visa, as he had been promised in Addis Ababa. The minister of education agreed to give us the visa with Bill's agreement that, in the future, we would start a school in the nearby town of Karen. However, instead of giving us a residence visa, they stamped our passports with a three-day exit visa. This meant that we had three days to leave Ethiopia or go to jail. Because of the war and the successful infiltration of Communism, they were not granting any more visas.

We were heart-broken. We felt that someone had kicked us in the stomach. I became literally ill and had to go to bed. How could this happen? Why had God permitted it? We felt that God had led us back to Ethiopia. We couldn't understand why this was happening. But we had to accept (Romans 8:28), "And we know that all things work together for good to them who love God, to them who are the called according to His purpose." This was somehow in God's purpose for us. Much later we learned that the town of Karen had been completely destroyed in the war. God certainly protects us, because He knows what lies ahead.

We had a lot to do before leaving the country. We immediately started packing the things that we wanted to ship from the country. The military men from the church said that they would ship our barrels of household goods after we were out of the country. We had to then decide what to take and what to leave behind. We had shipped all of our earthly possessions to the country in hopes that we would remain there the rest of our lives.

We quickly sorted and packed all the things that we had to take with us. Then we advertised by signs and word of mouth to the Ethiopians that we were selling everything. Because of the lack of things to buy in the country, people with money started knocking on our door. They wanted to buy before someone beat them to the things.

I was almost an emotional basket case as I showed prospective buyers around our house. We had to try to get a decent price for our things while going through the custom of bargaining over every item.

At the peak of my frustration, a couple of affluent Ethiopian women came to buy. When they started to leave, I noticed that one of them had a nice folding umbrella exactly like mine. Because of my mental state and the knowledge that we had to be very careful of thieves, I thought she was stealing my umbrella.

"You have my umbrella," I gently said to her.

She seemed surprised and replied, "No, this is my umbrella. I brought it with me."

I was insistent that it was mine (I had brought it from the States), and she was equally insistent that it was hers. Bill was frantic to prevent a fight, so he quickly started searching the house for my umbrella while we were arguing. To his relief and to my embarrassment, he found my umbrella. I could have died on the spot. I repeatedly apologized to the woman, but I'm afraid that she left thinking that I was totally insane. In the least, she felt offended that I had accused her of being a thief. I still regret that incident.

After three days, we had packed everything in barrels, except for the clothes in our suitcases. We sold all of the furniture, many of our personal things, and closed out the house. The servicemen had agreed to be responsible to sell our vehicle and send us the money. After saying an emotional goodbye to our friends, we were ready to board a plane to take us permanently from the country.

## We Again Said a Final Goodbye to Ethiopia

Bill never considered returning to the United States. He felt that God had called us to the mission field and since we couldn't remain in Ethiopia that he would accept the "Macedonian Call" that we received in Spain. We would proceed on to Australia. However, we had to have a visa.

Since we had to exit Ethiopia, we decided to fly to Nairobi, Kenya, where there was an Australian Embassy. We would apply for a visa and wait in Nairobi until it was issued. We had no idea what lay ahead in Kenya. At that time, the country wasn't open for our missionaries. It had only been a few short years since the bloody battle for independence there. We didn't know anyone in the country, but we knew God. We trusted Him to make the crooked paths straight for us. I understand a little of what Abraham must have felt when he was told to leave his home and go to a country that was totally foreign to him.

# CHAPTER 21

# The Long Wait for an Australian Visa

When we left the plane and walked into the terminal in Nairobi, we had no idea what was coming next. We had three small children, a limited supply of money, a few clothes, a lot of anxiety, but a lot of faith (and probably a lack of good sense).

We must have looked like lost sheep in a hailstorm as we stood inside the terminal trying to decide what to do next. But God always has someone prepared to help His children. Before long, an American couple (who worked for the Embassy) approached us and asked if we needed a ride into Nairobi. We gratefully said that we did. (Thank You, Lord.)

My nerves were still suffering, and the ride into the city didn't help them. I almost had a heart attack when we started down the highway on the wrong side of the road. I thought that crazy American was going to get us killed. I soon realized that we were in a former English colony, and they drove on the left side of the road. (We drove on the right in Ethiopia, even though Lonnie had a van with the steering wheel on the right.)

They asked us where we were going to spend the night, and we had to confess that we didn't know. We explained why we had suddenly left Ethiopia. They were very sympathetic and helpful (who wouldn't have been with such a destitute young family in their car?). They probably knew that we couldn't afford one of the luxury hotels, so they took us downtown to a small hotel and helped us to check in. We expressed our thanks to those kind strangers and to our heavenly Father who had brought us this far on our mystery journey.

We didn't get much sleep that night because the hotel was above a nightclub. The music and the noise continued through most of the night. We knew by morning that we had to make different arrangements.

## We Stayed in the Mennonite Guesthouse

While still in Ethiopia, we heard about a missionary guesthouse that was operated by the Mennonite Church. Some of the missionaries in Ethiopia had gone to Kenya for vacations and stayed there. We determined to try to find that guesthouse. It was a blessing that most of the Kenyans spoke English. When we inquired about Menno Guesthouse, we were given directions to it.

We took a taxi to the place. Soon we had secured a large room with full board on the beautiful, peaceful compound of the guesthouse. The buildings were originally built for British military officers during the World War. The rates were reasonable and the food was good. The room was designed for a family and had five beds and a private bathroom. It was simple, but we rejoiced that we were able to be there. We didn't realize that it would be our home for the next seven weeks.

We applied for our Australian visa, and they asked who would be sponsoring us into the country. The Australians did not react when we said that we didn't know anyone in the country. (We later learned that anyone who received a visa to live in Australia was required to have someone in the country to sponsor them and to take responsibility for them.) They were very kind, took our applications, and told us that they would call us. (I hate that statement.) We trusted God and completely believed that we would get the visa.

We relaxed at the guesthouse while the children enjoyed playing on the large, green lawn. There was a tree with low-hanging limbs that was safe for them to climb. They called it the monkey tree.

We enjoyed going into Nairobi and looking at all of the nice woodcarvings and handiwork of the Kenyans. We were surprised to see thousands of East Indians. The ladies looked so beautiful in their long, graceful saris. I almost felt that we were in India. We learned that the Indians had come to Kenya many years ago to help build the railroad. They had stayed and adopted Kenya as their home. I was very impressed with them.

We had great fellowship with many other missionaries who were staying at the guesthouse and enjoyed the mid-morning and mid-afternoon "tea time." It would have been a wonderful vacation if we had not been stressed about visas.

We went through a wildlife park where we saw many of the wild animals of Kenya. One experience stands out in my mind. We were walking through some jungle along a river. The kids were walking in front of us, and Shaleen was eating a cookie. Suddenly, a little monkey appeared from the bush. As quick as lightening, he ran up Shaleen's leg and grabbed the cookie from her hand. He went up her body, over her head, and jumped back into the trees. She was screaming and near hysteria as she stood frozen to the spot. She quickly threw down two other cookies that she held in her other hand. The monkey grabbed them and ran away.

Our environment was pleasant, but we grew very tired of waiting. It seems that we have been in God's waiting room so much of our lives. I am very impatient. God is always saying to me, "Be still, and know that I am God: I will be exalted among the heathen, I will be exalted in the earth" (Psalm 46:10). I hate to just be still and wait.

After we rested and our nerves had a chance to unwind, we grew weary. Week after week we would call the Embassy and get the same answer, "We haven't received any news yet. We'll call you."

## Thank God for Another Missionary

We bought an English newspaper one Saturday, and while looking in the advertisements (when you get bored enough you read everything), we saw a tiny announcement of a church service at the Independent Baptist Church of Thika. The phone number was there, so Bill called. To our surprise and delight, he talked to a Baptist missionary, Ed Weaver. Ed and his family had been forced out of Congo a few years prior when the war came there. They came into Kenya and started a church. He invited us to come to church the next day and to have lunch with them. He even offered to come into the city and pick us up in his van.

We enjoyed the church service and the fellowship with the Weavers. They invited us to leave the guesthouse and come to stay with them until we received our visas for Australia. We were thrilled to have this kind invitation. Ed took us back to the guesthouse, collected our luggage, and we moved to their house.

They had a daughter about the age of our daughters, and they enjoyed playing together. Bill enthusiastically helped Ed with the church work. Marie and I were taking advantage of fellowship that both of us had missed. She had experienced a lot of upset in leaving Congo and then lost a child in a road accident in Kenya. We comforted each other.

## Old Fears Still Hurt

One night we were sitting in the kitchen while the men were on visitation and the children were playing. We heard some noise outside the kitchen door. Marie tried to open the door, but something was holding it from the outside. She was still nervous from the war in Congo, and this visibly upset her. She thought someone was outside. I became a little nervous also because Kenya had certainly experienced much horror during the past war for independence.

We finally called one of her teenage sons who came and forced the door open. He found, to our relief and amusement, that some well-meaning Kenyan church member had hung a bag of potatoes on the door as a gift for the missionaries. The weight of the bag kept the door from opening. We felt a bit stupid for getting unnerved.

## Australia Wanted Us

After two weeks, we received a call from the Australian Embassy. They asked us to come to the visa office. We hurried down, and they stamped our passports with a permanent migrant visa for Australia. We were elated, and we thanked God for answering our prayers. It would be some time before we would realize that the stamps in those passports were truly a miracle from God.

We said goodbye to the Weavers and, with great excitement, boarded a plane that would take us to Australia. As I sat on the plane waiting for take-off, my mind was in turmoil. I was happy that our long waiting time in Kenya was over, but what did the future hold?

We were going to a strange country where we didn't know one person. No one would be at the airport to greet us. Where would we stay? How would we even temporarily live on our very limited funds? We had spent most of our money (from the sale of our possessions) in Kenya. How would we rent a house or buy a car with no money? Since rented houses were very limited in Australia, how would we even find a house? If we were able to find a house, how would we set up housekeeping? All we had with us was our clothing. It would be months before our personal household things would arrive from Ethiopia. We had three small children, one ready to start to school; what would we do?

I had no choice but to trust my husband and my God. God had promised that He would never leave us nor forsake us. He was God in Australia as much as in America or Africa. He would be with us and take care of us regardless of what the future would hold. Our future was in God's hands.

I didn't know what I would experience in the next weeks, months, and years in that strange "land down under." I now thank God that I didn't know.

*Also available from Pleasant Word: Follow LaMoin Cunningham and her family through their amusing and lively adventures as missionaries adjusting to yet another foreign culture, Australia, in her next book:* I'm Glad I Didn't Know!

To order additional copies of

# Oh, Lord,

# What
# Have I
# Gotten
# Myself
# Into?

## FOR ADDITIONAL COPIES
Mail $18.00 (includes s/h) to:
LaMoin Cunningham
P.O. Box 804
Talbott, TN 37877
Email: LaMoinBill@aol.com

Printed in the United States
122338LV00001B/82-129/A